To order prints or books visit:
www.jarviedigital.com/Temples

American Temples

of The Church of Jesus Christ of Latter-day Saints

A Faith in America Production by

Scott Jarvie

Washington D.C. Temple

Research and Design
Aubriahna Greene

Production Editor
Kimberly Tweed

Copy Editor
Karen Hyatt

Story Editors
Jenna Anderson
Aubriahna Greene
Ashlee Jessen
Beau Sorensen

Authors
Kayla Abilez
Denise Allen

D. Anderson
Jason Bagley
Austin Baird
Elaine Barnett
Kathleen Bingham
Connor Boyack
Becky Busath
Shay Carl Butler
Bernadene A. Carter
Sharron Clevenstine
Kaylene Myres Coleman
Carri Cozzens
Richard Doutre'Jones
Meredith Ethington
Monica Franco-Rivera
Rachel Whitaker Galbraith

Kristin Garvin
Izabela Geambașu
Eivonny Yvonne Grimske
Carrie Greene
Carmen Rasmusen Herbert
Karen Hyatt
Liz Jensen
Kayla Lemmon
Derek Lines
Deanna Moulton
Alex J. Olson
Benjeline Misalucha Quirante
Celeste Reed
Shelbee Ropte
Danielle Self
Beau Sorensen

David Steenhoek
Lindsey Stirling
Ben Toney
Maria Luisa Vasquez
James Voss
Stephen Weber
Daniel Wilkes
Rebecca Brown Wright

Websites
ldschurchtemples.com
mormontemples.com
ldschurchnewsarchive.com
deseretnews.com
mormonnewsroom.org

ISBN: 978-0-9908681-0-1

Salt Lake City Utah Temple

Scott Jarvie, Photographer

Scott studied languages at BYU, and while traveling in Europe he discovered his love for photography. He has spent the last decade and tens of thousands of hours fervently honing his craft. Scott is a full-time photographer, earning a living primarily as a wedding photographer, while still getting plenty of opportunities to travel the world.

Introduction

This Wasn't the Plan

Life doesn't always seem to go the way you plan. And there is often beauty in that. The beauty is manifest when you accept those times and make the best of them.

Until recently, I would never have envisioned myself making this book for you. I didn't plan on photographing all 70 U.S. temples of The Church of Jesus Christ of Latter-day Saints or becoming a photographer known for pictures of LDS temples. I didn't start to focus on temple pictures until about three years ago, when I was on a cross-country road trip and decided it would give me focal points to stop at. I was a wedding, portrait, and travel photographer, not an architecture enthusiast, but it's not a bad twist to the story of my life. It has become a worthwhile and uplifting endeavor that has improved me as a photographer and as a person.

I did not even have this book in mind at the beginning of 2013, when I set off for this year-long adventure. My decision to live on the road for a year and visit all 50 states is a story with a long string of events that some may call "coincidences" and others may call "opportunities." These events, guised as random decisions, ended up shaping my future career and passion.

The Making of a Book

In March of 2013, I went on a road trip to photograph the American Southwest, and somewhere between the Grand Canyon and the Utah border I had "one of those days." The kind of day that takes a crazy turn. The kind of day where one minute everything is peachy, you haven't got a care in the world, and you're content with life – and the next minute something has changed. It's as if God says, "I see you're satisfied…don't be!"

I didn't take off on that two-week road trip for the purpose of self reflection or to figure things out, but simply to fulfill the itch of photography and to see new places. I was happy, my career was going well, but inside my heart was placed a seed of desire to do more, and I suddenly sensed a big hole in my life. Fortunately, there were three large projects I'd been thinking about for years, and that day I poured my heart out in prayer, right there on the empty desert roads, because I wanted God's help figuring out the next big step and which of these ideas I should pursue.

I thought about them all day and into the next, trying to decide which project to take on, when a

If you can see ahead of you every step of the way, then there is no need for that faith which enables you to step out into the dark…

little idea began to creep in. For the rest of the trip it was all I could think of. That little thought placed in my mind was not one of the original three ideas. It was something new that I'd never considered. Something I would have laughed away just days before. Something that had even been suggested by a friend previously but that I had

Brigham City Utah Temple

rejected as an impossibility: What about making a temple book?

An Idea Takes Shape

I spent all day considering whether it was something I should do. It just seemed right. It was an answer to a prayer. Even though there were other options that would have been easier or seemingly more enjoyable, I decided to do it, and I never looked back. I spent the next three months trying to figure out how to make it happen, and the answers started to flow into my mind: crowd funding, Kickstarter, trailer, all 50 states, books, pre-sales, etc.

The project grew and, within a few weeks, had evolved from photographing 70 LDS temples to photographing buildings of every religion in all 50 states, leading to the creation of *two* books: one highlighting LDS temples, and the other focusing on faith in America.

This book, *American Temples*, remains the primary reason and the inspiration for the road trip. The inspiration from that single day of clarity in the high desert of Arizona is what kept me going through months of planning, even when it seemed things wouldn't work out – and especially heading into the last few hours of what appeared to be a failed funding campaign.

Laie Hawaii Temple

Trial of Faith

I had spent months of planning and was 29.5 days into a 30-day, all-or-nothing Kickstarter crowd funding campaign. I had spent hundreds of hours on it and had the assistance and confidence of hundreds of people; yet if I didn't receive the necessary funds within just a few hours, it would not happen. I wondered why I had been prompted to do a project when it seemed I wouldn't have the money or means to complete it.

Even on that final day, however, I was committed to the idea of getting out on the road and trying. Perhaps it wasn't going to be exactly like I had envisioned, but I was still going to do what I could, even if it meant just getting out there for a month or two until the money ran out or I figured out something else.

I think that faith isn't really faith unless it's tried. If you can see ahead of you every step of the way, then there is no need for that faith which enables you to step out into the dark. When everything makes total sense and seems to be going perfectly, it's not faith that guides your step. I saw this firsthand as my faith was tried. With only a few hours to raise more money than I had raised in the previous 29.5 days, and when things seemed 100% impossible, it was then that faith was proven substantive and played an active role.

It was as if God was saying, "I know you're willing to do what I tell you as long as everything makes perfect sense and seems enjoyable and interesting and it's all paid for, but what will you do when it starts becoming more work than fun and nothing is paid for and it seems entirely impossible?"

It was after this moment that I realized things could work out in a way other than what I had planned. And then the miracle came.

A Way Was Provided

I was certain about what I should do at that moment of answered prayer back in March, and I believed in the feeling and assurance of that moment. So despite the change of plans, I resigned myself to the idea of doing what I could with what I had. Little did I know that in the background God was inspiring a friend, through a random series of events, to be on the right TV channel at the right moment to see me on a news interview. This led to his offering to use my talents and this project to help his company obtain some needed pictures from around the United States. In just a few short hours, what had seemed impossible had happened. The project was funded, and I had all I needed to set out on this journey.

Every day I have been reminded in small ways that I can make all the plans I want, but I should really appreciate when God steps in and the unexpected turns become an amazing experience that no amount of planning would have provided me.

Now I'm sitting here in a car with my metaphorical finish line in sight, and I am again contemplating what is next with the same feelings, wondering what's in store, feeling nervous and excited.

I have a lot of ideas, but one thing I've learned is that no matter how good your ideas, the best idea is the one the Spirit of God directs you to do, and when the answer comes…have faith.

– *Scott Jarvie*

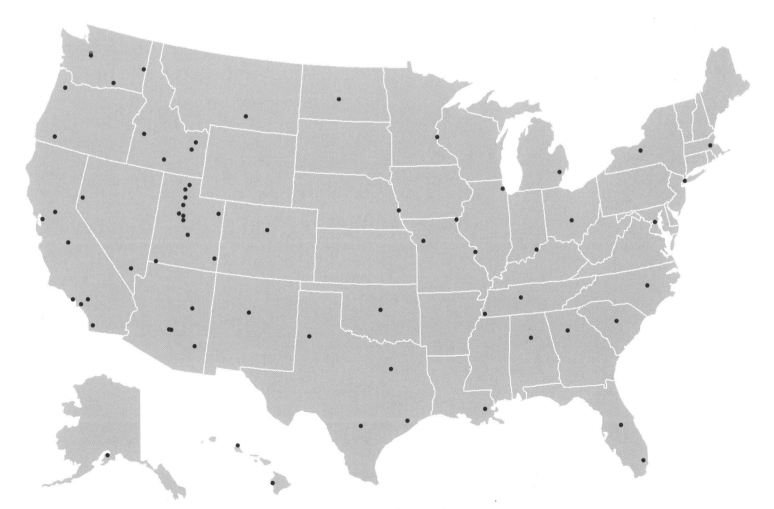

Map of all 70 completed U.S. temples of The Church of Jesus Christ of Latter-day Saints.

Table of Contents
Organized by Dedication Date

1850 – 1899

St. George Utah	12
Logan Utah	16
Manti Utah	22
Salt Lake City Utah	28

1900 – 1949

Laie Hawaii	34
Mesa Arizona	38
Idaho Falls Idaho	42

1950 – 1999

Los Angeles California	46
Oakland California	52
Ogden Utah	58
Provo Utah	62
Washington D.C.	66
Seattle Washington	72
Jordan River Utah	76
Atlanta Georgia	80
Boise Idaho	84
Dallas Texas	88
Chicago Illinois	92
Denver Colorado	96
Portland Oregon	100
Las Vegas Nevada	104
San Diego California	110
Orlando Florida	116
Bountiful Utah	120
Mount Timpanogos Utah	124
St. Louis Missouri	130
Vernal Utah	134
Monticello Utah	138
Anchorage Alaska	140
Spokane Washington	144
Columbus Ohio	146
Bismarck North Dakota	148
Columbia South Carolina	150
Detroit Michigan	152
Billings Montana	154
Raleigh North Carolina	158

2000 – Present

St. Paul Minnesota	160	Snowflake Arizona	214
Kona Hawaii	162	Lubbock Texas	216
Albuquerque New Mexico	166	Nauvoo Illinois	218
Louisville Kentucky	170	Redlands California	224
Palmyra New York	172	Manhattan New York	226
Fresno California	178	San Antonio Texas	228
Medford Oregon	180	Newport Beach California	230
Memphis Tennessee	184	Sacramento California	234
Reno Nevada	186	Rexburg Idaho	238
Nashville Tennessee	190	Twin Falls Idaho	242
Baton Rouge Louisiana	192	Draper Utah	246
Oklahoma City Oklahoma	196	Oquirrh Mountain Utah	250
Houston Texas	198	Gila Valley Arizona	254
Birmingham Alabama	202	Kansas City Missouri	258
Boston Massachusetts	204	Brigham City Utah	262
Winter Quarters Nebraska	208	Gilbert Arizona	266
Columbia River Washington	212	Fort Lauderdale Florida	270

Extras

Payson Utah	274
Kirtland Ohio	275
Canadian Temples	276
Index	278

St. George Utah

Announcement:	November 9, 1871
Dedication:	April 6-8, 1877 by Daniel H. Wells
Rededication:	November 11-12, 1975
Site:	6 acres
Floor Area:	110,000 square feet
Exterior Finish:	Native red sand stone quarried north of the city and plastered white

A Long-Awaited Temple

The St. George Temple was the first temple completed after the Latter-day Saints migrated from Nauvoo. As a result, it got a lot of special attention from Brigham Young. As President George A. Smith said, "you cannot realize how...anxious [Brigham Young] is to get this temple completed. He feels he is getting old and is liable to drop off at any time and he has keys that he wants to give in that temple that can only be given in a temple" ("Journal and Diary of Robert Gardner," *Heart Throbs of the West*, 10:321).

One of the key individuals involved in the building of the St. George Temple was my ancestor Robert Gardner. Robert was called to lead the United Order in St. George and got the sawmill working on Mount Trumbull, over 70 miles away from St. George, in order to provide lumber for the temple. Before Brigham Young asked him to get the sawmill working, they had spent six months with almost no lumber cut or transported to the temple site for construction. After he was called to supervise the collection of the lumber, the job was done in less than six months.

Robert worked regularly on the temple. To quote from his journal, "My time had been all taken up from the time the Temple commenced to be built until the roof was on. I had helped in getting material together for repairing roads, getting the rock from the quarries, seeing to shelter and other things needed for the men that were called from the outside settlements. Most of the time we had over two hundred men employed. I was among the first to superintend making the road to get the rock to lay the foundation and the last to furnish the lumber to put on the roof and finish the inside work."

As a result of their selfless service, the St. George Temple was dedicated on January 1, 1877 – eight months before Brigham Young died.

Every time I go to St. George, I love entering the city from the south via I-15. As you go up over the rise you can see the stark whiteness of the temple contrasted with the brilliant red of the surrounding cliffs. I think of the challenges associated with the construction of the temple – construction crews working in over 100-degree temperatures; men and oxen hauling loads of lumber 70 miles each way; men pulling 5,500-pound slabs of volcanic rock down the side of a mountain to create the foundation for the House of the Lord. Then I feel gratitude for their faith in the Lord and in His work. I am grateful to be a descendant of people like Robert Gardner who truly gave all that they had to the building up of Zion.

– Beau Sorensen, Utah

> *I love entering the city from the south…as you go up over the rise you can see the stark whiteness of the temple contrasted with the brilliant red of the surrounding cliffs.*

Interesting Facts

- The St. George Utah Temple is the oldest operating temple of the Church.

- The St. George Utah Temple is the only temple completed during Brigham Young's 30-year tenure as president of the Church.

- In November 1928, a fire destroyed the St. George Utah Temple annex. All records and furnishings were saved. Today's annex was constructed in the 1950s and serves as the entrance to the temple.

Logan Utah

Announcement:	October 6, 1876
Dedication:	May 17-19, 1884 by John Taylor
Rededication:	March 13-15, 1979
Site:	9 acres
Floor Area:	119,619 square feet
Exterior Finish:	Dark siliceous limestone

From the *Church News*

Called to help build the Logan Utah Temple as a young father, Rasmus Julius Smith would walk 22 miles from Brigham City to Logan every Monday morning, work for the week, and then make the trek home on Saturday. While in this calling, he worked as a hod carrier, a worker who carried mortar or plaster on his shoulders to the masons working on the temple. His devoted wife, Josephine, cared for their family, home, property and animals while her husband was away. He did this each week for almost two years. At the conclusion of his service in 1884, a letter was issued certifying he had "worked faithfully and honorably on the Logan temple for nearly two years." After the temple was completed, his service continued with years of family history work and time spent in the temple.

"Can you imagine walking all that way and then going to work on the temple?" said Elder Allan F. Packer, a great-grandson of Rasmus Smith and member of the Seventy. "Our ancestor did that for just about two years… He responded to the call and did it because he had a testimony in his heart and mind."

Sister Donna Smith Packer, wife of President Boyd K. Packer, President of the Quorum of the Twelve, said she cherishes the faithful example her grandfather set for his posterity.

"My grandfather, Rasmus Julius Smith, led a productive and fruitful life," she said. "He was known for his patience, honesty and thrift. His energetic devotion was to his family as well as to The Church of Jesus Christ of Latter-day Saints. How do I know this since I was under two years of age when he passed away, August 7, 1929? I know this because of his works, the temple records he left to us as his posterity and because of my personal witness of the Spirit."[1]

Interesting Facts

- The five-story Logan Utah Temple was built entirely by volunteers over a seven-year period from 1877 to 1884.

- The exterior walls of the temple were originally painted an off-white to hide the rough limestone. In the early 1900s, the paint was allowed to weather away, uncovering the beautiful stone that characterizes the temple today.

- On the evening of December 4, 1917, a fire started, engulfing the southeast staircase, destroying several windows and paintings, and causing extensive smoke and water damage. The origin of the fire was discovered to be electrical wiring.

- The Logan Utah Temple was floodlit at night for the first time during the month of May 1934 as part of the temple's Golden Jubilee celebration. Thirteen years would pass before the temple was lit again on the temple's 63rd anniversary – now with a permanent system.

- The Logan Utah Temple is the only temple to be completely gutted and rebuilt inside. The two-year project replaced the progressive-style ordinance rooms with motion-picture ordinance rooms. President Spencer W. Kimball, who rededicated the completed temple in 1979, regretted the need to reconstruct the interior because of the loss of pioneer craftsmanship.

Manti Utah

Announcement:	June 25, 1875
Dedication:	May 21-23, 1888 by Lorenzo Snow
Rededication:	June 14-16, 1985 by Gordon B. Hinckley
Site:	27 acres
Floor Area:	100,373 square feet
Exterior finish:	Cream oolite limestone from the hill on which it stands

I'm Going There Someday

Long before the Primary song "I Love to See the Temple" was written, I first saw the Manti Temple as a child, and I remember thinking to myself, "I am going there someday." The Manti Temple is the temple of my ancestors. My great-grandfather was the first sheriff in that area when there were American Indians living on the land. My great-uncle was also in the temple presidency, and my husband and I were privileged to have him as our sealer on our wedding day.

My husband and I actually eloped to the temple, in part because no family members at the time were temple-goers. The next time we were able to go back to the temple was twenty years later for the Sesquicentennial celebration. We were given a personal tour and got to see and enjoy areas of the temple that newlyweds would never have noticed on their special day.

— *Denise Allen, Texas*

Interesting Facts

- The Manti Temple is home to the annual outdoor "Mormon Miracle Pageant," attended by nearly 100,000 guests.

- The Manti Utah Temple is one of two temples that still use live acting for presentation of the endowment. The other is the Salt Lake Temple.

- Lightning struck the east tower of the Manti Utah Temple in 1928, which started a fire that burned for three hours before it could be extinguished.

- In 1985, the Manti Utah Temple was formally rededicated following a four-year renovation project that included updating the auxiliary systems of the temple; adding three sealing rooms, new dressing rooms, a nursery, and offices; and restoring the pioneer craftsmanship and artwork to their former glory. The three-day open house was attended by over 40,000 visitors.

Salt Lake City Utah

Announcement:	July 28, 1847
Dedication:	April 6-24, 1893 by Wilford Wooduff
Site:	10 acres
Floor Area:	253,000 square feet
Exterior Finish:	Quartz monzonite quarried from Little Cottonwood Canyon, 20 miles southeast of Salt Lake City

To Walk Where the Savior has Walked

"And it shall come to pass in the last days, that the mountain of the Lord's house shall be established in the top of the mountains, and shall be exalted above the hills; and all nations shall flow unto it" (Isaiah 2:2).

These were my thoughts when I first saw the Salt Lake Temple in person. I remember having a picture of it ever since I was baptized and wishing that one day I could go there. Little did I know then that after just a year of being baptized I would receive a mission call to serve right at the feet of what I have come to call "my temple." I still remember walking up to it for the first time and being filled with the Spirit of the Lord! How could I ever describe in words the Salt Lake Temple and my mission right at at its feet – the Utah Salt Lake City Temple Square Mission.

My first Mission President, Richard I. Winwood, had a rule for us Temple Square sisters. On our preparation day, instead of our three hours of proselytizing, he told us to go to the temple. So throughout my mission I was able to go to the temple weekly – what a great blessing! How I wish I could have a way of doing that still, but now the closest temple to me is 12 hours away…But, how grateful I am for the inspired rule of President Winwood. Because of it, I have come to appreciate the temple for its real value. Going to the temple weekly brought special insights of knowledge and revelation that are too sacred for me to share, but I testify that the temple is the House of the Lord and our safe haven on earth. If we appreciate it for its worth, if we go there prepared from every point of view and if we visit it so often that it becomes our second home, it will be to us what the Salt Lake Temple has become to me: my fortress, my princess fairy tale castle, my tower of strength, my beacon of light. How I wish I could climb its stairs again and feel of its spirit!

I will forever be grateful for the chance I have had to walk where the Savior has walked!

– Izabela Geambaşu (aka Sister Ţicală),
Oradea, Romania

Interesting Facts

- Though its construction was begun first, the Salt Lake Temple was the fourth temple built in Utah.
- Original plans for the Salt Lake Temple called for two angel Moroni statues – one on the east central spire and one on the west.
- The Salt Lake Temple took 40 years to build, with its highly ornate interior being completed in just a year.
- The walls of the Salt Lake Temple are nine feet thick at the base and six feet thick at the top.
- The Salt Lake Temple is one of two temples that still uses live acting for presentation of the endowment. The other is the Manti Utah Temple.

A Forever Room

I was sitting cross-legged on my living room floor when I saw a picture of the Salt Lake Temple for the first time. I was looking up at a young man with a name tag who had come all the way from Missouri to knock on doors and tell us families can be together forever. Taking the picture from him, I still remember saying, "I'm going to get married there."

Four years later I stood in the bride's room of the Salt Lake Temple, zipping up the back of my dress and touching one of my curls lightly. I remembered back to when this castle was simply a picture on a postcard. It was the place that was part of "someday." After my baptism, four years of college, countless weddings of friends, and walks around the temple grounds imagining what the sealing room looked like, I was finally here. I had pictured the chandelier, the white velvet on the altar, and the paintings of Christ. I imagined the flowers and the vases and the pristine stained glass. I looked forward to seeing the intricate carvings that told the story of the forty years it took to complete, and the brass doorknobs that have been touched by generations of Saints before me. I imagined that would be the most amazing part. Looking back, I realize I was wrong.

It was my Dad, suited up with a blue tie and a full head of hair, eyes smiling as I came in the room, that made it beautiful. Little did I know I'd retrace that memory over and over in later years after my Dad slipped to the other side of the veil.

It was my sister-in-law that made it beautiful, with her arms temporarily free of her squirming kids, who winked at me over my husband's shoulder that day, inviting me into her heart. Only a few months later we lost her as well, but she's alive for me in that moment.

It was my Mom with tissue in her hands, my friends from every corner of my life, my professor from BYU-Idaho, and the missionary who taught me the gospel, lining the walls that day. It outshined the beauty I had imagined. It was the hugs, the smiles, the whispers of "I love you" that stand out more than any stained glass or castle door. It was the few minutes where time stopped, death waited, and so did life – there was just forever in that room.

To some, it may seem ordinary to be surrounded by the people who make up your life – the ones who might never share the same room again. But to me – even now, years later and hundreds of miles away from those temple doors – that moment was more beautiful and more extraordinary than anything I'd ever seen.

– Kayla Lemmon, Washington
lemmonythings.com

> *I remembered back to when this castle was simply a picture on a postcard. It was the place that was part of "someday."*

Laie Hawaii

Announcement:	October 3, 1915
Dedication:	November 27-30, 1919 by Heber J. Grant
Rededication:	June 13-15, 1978
Site:	11.4 acres
Floor Area:	47,224 square feet
Exterior Finish:	Concrete made from native lava rock and coral, reinforced with steel; the outside layer is pneumatic stone

Interesting Facts

- President Joseph F. Smith was in Hawaii on business in the spring of 1915 when he was moved by a spiritual impulse to dedicate a site for the Laie Hawaii Temple. That action was later ratified by the Brethren and publicly sustained in the October 1915 General Conference.

- Construction of the Laie Hawaii Temple came to a standstill when the supply of lumber ran out. Prayers were uttered, and two days later, a freighter was discovered stranded on a nearby coral reef. The captain offered his entire cargo to the Saints if they would unload it for him. His cargo? Lumber – enough to complete the temple.

- In May 1976, the Laie Hawaii Temple closed for two years for extensive remodeling that provided a new front entrance, enlarged the patron and administrative facilities, and converted the progressive-style ordinance rooms to stationary ordinance rooms equipped for motion-picture presentation of the endowment.

Mesa Arizona

Announcement:	October 3, 1919
Dedication:	October 23-26, 1927, by Heber J. Grant
Rededication:	April 15-16, 1975
Site:	20 acres
Floor Area:	133,916 square feet
Exterior Finish:	Concrete and steel dressed with colored terra cotta tiles

Interesting Facts

- The Mesa Arizona Temple was the first temple to present the endowment in a language other than English when it held the first Spanish session in 1945.

- Instead of a formal open house, tours were offered during the last two years of construction of the Mesa Arizona Temple to any interested visitors.

- Carved friezes decorate each corner of the top of the temple, depicting the fulfillment of Isaiah's prophecy that the Lord would gather His people in the last days from the four corners of the earth.

I Didn't Lead You to Fall

My love for the temple started when I attended for the first time, in the Mesa Temple. When I'm in the temple, it's almost as if I can look at my life through different eyes. I feel like I get a glimpse of God's plan for me, and all the worries and stresses of life suddenly aren't that important. In the temple, the walls are white, the decor is simple, clean and elegant, and there is a tangible peace. When I'm in the temple I find it so much easier to listen to God.

Not long ago I was feeling almost suffocated by the pressures in my life, to the point where my fear was crippling my progression. I went to the temple and as I sat in the quiet solace, I heard an inaudible voice say to me very clearly, "I did not lead you this far to let you fall." I was immediately filled with so much love – *so much love*. And the confidence I had lost came back. In that instant, I knew as clearly as I know anything that God was aware of me and He was going to inspire me. I was not in this alone; I'd never been alone. Everything was so clear as I sat there in the temple. Through the next few months I leaned heavily on the memory of that moment, and it carried me through.

– *Lindsey Stirling*

Idaho Falls Idaho

Announcement:	November 9, 1871
Dedication:	April 6–8, 1877
	by Daniel H. Wells
Rededication:	November 11-12, 1975
Site:	6 acres
Floor Area:	110,000 square feet
Exterior Finish:	Native red sand stone from north of the city and plastered white

Where Families Are Built

The Idaho Falls temple is the most important building in the world! This is not because the design, architecture, landscaping, or furnishings are superior to any of the other thousands of beautiful religious edifices that have been constructed since the beginning of our species.

It's the most important building in the world to me because that is where my family began. Within those four sacred walls an eternal relationship with the girl of my dreams was created. Because of that relationship I was blessed to become a father and learn that true happiness comes from loving someone more than you love yourself. Temples are where families are built and families can be together forever and the things that matter most last the longest.

– Shay Butler, Idaho

Los Angeles California

Announcement:	March 6, 1937
Dedication:	March 11–14, 1956 by David O. McKay
Site:	13 acres
Floor Area:	190,614 square feet
Exterior Finish:	Mo-Sai stone, crushed quartz and white Portland cement

A Refuge from the World

I first received my own endowments when I was preparing to serve a mission in Anaheim, California. I was able to attend the temple only a handful of times while at the Missionary Training Center in Provo, Utah, learning the Spanish language, so once I was in the mission field, it was such a treat to get to go to the temple again. The temple we were assigned to for our mission was the Los Angeles Temple. Since it was about an hour and a half away, we only were able to go twice a year as missionaries.

I remember the first time I went to the Los Angeles Temple. I had been serving as a missionary in some of the not-so-nice areas of my mission and was anxious to feel that special temple Spirit again. We drove to Los Angeles in a bus full of missionaries, and sang hymns and watched a spiritual video on the way. The temple is in an area of L.A. that is very urban, and the temple definitely sticks out on the hill it is set on. I remember feeling so peaceful once I stepped onto those temple grounds, despite the busy city that we could see below us. Once I stepped inside, the Spirit was even stronger.

I was grateful that day to attend the temple with so many fellow missionaries, to be taught by the temple presidency, and to have a few hours to relish the Spirit you can feel there. It was a way to recharge as a missionary and stay focused on a work that is so important. When we left the temple, I remember the stark contrast I felt looking at the city down below, and in that moment, I received a confirmation that the temple is a refuge from the world.

I'm so grateful for the temple in my

> *When we left the temple, I remember the stark contrast I felt looking at the city down below, and in that moment I received a confirmation that the temple is a refuge from the world.*

life today, too. As a missionary, it was important to attend the temple, but I know it plays an even more vital role in my life today as a refuge against the outside world, recharging me for my most important job as a mom to three little ones, and strengthening my relationship with my husband, and more importantly, my Heavenly Father. I grew up in Texas, almost two hours away from the nearest temple, and feel extremely blessed to live in Utah now and have access to so many temples around me. I know that the temple is the house of God and is meant to be a refuge to escape the trials and worries we face in this life.

– Meredith Ethington, Utah
perfectionpending.net

A Beacon of Faith

The Los Angeles Temple has always been a beacon of hope and faith for me. I remember the first time I went to the temple to do baptisms for the dead. It was a very awe-inspiring moment of my young life. Every time I'd rise out of the water I'd see the large painting of Christ being baptized by John the Baptist. I could feel that what I was doing was good and had worth.

As I grew older, I received a call to serve as a missionary in the Brazil Campinas Mission. It was the Los Angeles Temple I turned toward once again, this time to receive my endowments.

It's amazing to me how this massive structure sits on one of the busiest streets in the world, Santa Monica Blvd., beckoning people to come visit and learn more. After my mission, I had opportunities to serve at the Los Angeles Temple in different ways, including putting up Christmas lights and being a part of the volunteer group of Saints to clean the different rooms inside the temple.

The most important day I experienced at the Los Angeles Temple was the day I was married for time and all eternity. It seems the Los Angeles Temple has always been there for me as a refuge and a home away from home. I hope to have many more firsts inside its walls as my children grow up near this sacred edifice.

– *David Steenhoek, California*

Oakland California

Announcement: January 23, 1961

Dedication: November 17-19, 1964
by David O. McKay

Site: 18.3 acres

Floor Area: 95,000 square feet

Exterior Finish: Concrete and Sierra white granite
from Raymond, California

Forever Family

I was a young, 21-year-old bride-to-be. I had met the love of my life and was engaged to be married. I had been prayerful in my decision to accept him as my eternal companion. We both had grown up in the San Francisco Bay area, making the Oakland Temple "our temple." As the day came for me to receive my own endowment, I unexpectedly became terrified of this eternal choice I was about to make. I went to my Father in Heaven and asked Him why I was so terrified now, even after receiving several confirmations that Clint was the right person for me to be sealed to. I felt that I should continue on and that I was on the right path. Surprising to me, though, I was still very nervous.

The morning came for me to receive my own

As moments come when we miss our son Jacob terribly, how thankful we are for that beautiful day in June when we were sealed as an eternal family...

endowment and enter the temple with my fiancé to prepare for our sealing. As I entered the endowment room, I sat down and glanced over at my sweet husband-to-be. As I did this, the Spirit filled my body from the top of my head to my toes. I felt a beautiful love and an assurance that he was to be my husband for now and for eternity. We have now been married

for 33 years. Our lives have been filled with both joy and sorrow.

We have been blessed with five beautiful children. We have endured the sorrow of the death of our second child, our son Jacob, at the tender age of four years. As we continue on, that wonderful day of our marriage in the Oakland Temple means more to us now than it did when we were only 21 and 23 years old. Our boy has moved on ahead to his Father in Heaven. As the moments come when we miss our son Jacob terribly, how thankful we are for that beautiful day in June when we were sealed as an eternal family, which now includes each one of our beautiful children, born in the covenant of our eternal marriage.

–Carrie Greene, Utah

Interesting Facts

- In 1942, the site for the Oakland California Temple was purchased after 14 years of negotiations.

- The temple in Oakland had been long awaited. It was in 1924 that Elder George Albert Smith, a member of the Quorum of the Twelve Apostles, saw a vision in which a great white temple stood in the Oakland hills. Construction, however, did not start until 1961.

- The temple is so prominent that ships entering San Francisco Bay use it as a navigation landmark.

- President Heber J. Grant announced the purchase of the site for the Oakland California Temple in the April 1943 General Conference: "I am happy to tell you that we have purchased in the Oakland area another temple site. The negotiations have been finally concluded and the title has passed. The site is located on the lower foothills of East Oakland on a rounded hill overlooking San Francisco Bay. We shall in due course build there a splendid temple."

Elder George Albert Smith of the Council of the Twelve envisioned that one day "a Temple would surmount the East Bay hills, one that would be visible as a beacon to ships as they entered the Golden Gate from the far-flung nations of the earth."

-David O. McKay

Ogden Utah

Announcement: August 24, 1967

Dedication: January 18-20, 1972
by Joseph Fielding Smith

Rededication: September 21, 2014

Site: 9.96 acres

Floor Area: 112,232 square feet

Exterior Finish: Granite

Interesting Facts

- The announcement of the Ogden and Provo Utah Temples was prompted by a statistic computed in the mid-1960s that 52 percent of all ordinance work was performed in three temples: the Logan Utah Temple, the Manti Utah Temple, and the Salt Lake Temple.

- At the dedication of the Ogden Utah Temple, President Harold B. Lee finished the remaining one-third of the dedicatory prayer when President Joseph Fielding Smith became too weak from standing so long.

- Ground was broken for the Ogden Utah Temple on the 96th birthday of President David O. McKay. He passed away just four months later. The temple was subsequently dedicated on the second anniversary of his passing.

Provo Utah

Announcement: August 14, 1967

Dedication: February 9, 1972
by Joseph Fielding Smith
read by Harold B. Lee

Site: 17 acres

Floor Area: 128,325 square feet

Exterior Finish: White cast stone, gold
anodized aluminum grills,
bronze glass panels

Serving in His House

I remember in January of 1972, when I was a teenager, going to the Provo Temple open house and looking forward to the day when I could attend the temple as a patron. That day finally arrived in 1981, when I was called to serve a mission and went to the Missionary Training Center in Provo. Once a week we were able to attend the beautiful Provo Temple as missionaries before entering the mission field.

Now, over 30 years later, I have the opportunity and blessing of being an ordinance worker at this same temple. Every Wednesday evening I have the opportunity of training sisters to be ordinance workers and to serve the patrons. I treasure these experiences. What a wonderful blessing it is to be able to serve in the House of the Lord, to feel of His presence, and to walk the halls where the Lord and Savior has indeed walked.

– Kathleen Bingham, Utah

Interesting Facts

- President Joseph Fielding Smith presided at the dedication of the Provo Utah Temple, but at his request, the prayer he had written was offered by President Harold B. Lee, first counselor in the First Presidency.
- The Provo Utah Temple was dedicated in just two sessions by seating the attendees not only in the temple, but also in the Marriott Center, the George Albert Smith Fieldhouse, the Joseph Smith Building, and the Harris Fine Arts Center on the BYU campus. In this way, over 70,000 people attended what was then the largest temple dedication in history.

Washington D.C.

Announcement: November 15, 1968

Dedication: November 19-22, 1974
by Spencer W. Kimball

Site: 52 acres

Floor Area: 160,000 square feet

Exterior Finish: Reinforced concrete sheeted in
Alabama white marble

Interesting Facts

- At a height of 288 feet, the Washington D.C. Temple is the tallest temple in the Church.

- The Washington D.C. Temple is one of five temples featuring a statue of the angel Moroni holding the gold plates. The other four are the Los Angeles California Temple, Jordan River Utah Temple, Seattle Washington Temple, and México City México Temple.

- The seven floors of the Washington D.C. Temple represent the six days of creation and the seventh day of rest.

- The highly successful public open house of the Washington D.C. Temple was attended by 758,328 guests, including special guest Betty Ford, wife of former president Gerald Ford. These tours resulted in over 75,000 missionary referrals.

Oma's Balcony

The Washington D.C. Temple has always been a hallowed sanctuary, a place where I have felt the peace and love of the Lord. It became more of a sacred refuge, a place that felt even more like home, after my dear grandma, who I called "Oma," passed away.

She and I had been so close, and what had really brought us together when I was about 12 years old was family history work. She was so passionate about performing that sacred work, and her dedication and unfailing commitment was contagious. She and I shared countless hours working together, compiling the history of our ancestors. Her health struggles later confined her to a nursing home, but our sweet relationship continued through precious visits I will always cherish.

After I moved out to D.C., she had a stroke, and I flew back for one last visit. On the way out, I was not sure whether I was flying out to see her or to attend her funeral, but thankfully we had a few days of sweet visits together. Even though she was unable to speak, her eyes still conveyed her deep love. Just before I had to leave again, I had a few minutes alone with her. I pulled her well-worn copy of the Book of Mormon off the shelf by her bed and read to her from Alma about what happens to the spirits of the righteous when they depart this life, and the blessed and happy state into which they enter. I told her how much I loved her, and then told her it was okay to go. I will never forget the look in her eyes; her tears of sadness at our rapidly approaching separation mixed with such love conveyed the message her voice was no longer able to.

Our shared testimony and sure witness of what awaited her, and the joyous reunion we would later have, provided peace despite the agony of the separation. After I had to return to D.C., she passed away peacefully. I was unable to return for the funeral, but I knew where she would want me to be: in the temple.

Every time I go to the D.C. Temple, my eyes are still drawn to Oma's balcony, half expecting to see her smiling down.

Her family – living and deceased – was what she had dedicated her entire life to, and I knew she would want me to continue that work.

As I sat in the celestial room, I felt my eyes drawn upward. There is a balcony that rings the room, and without meaning to, my eyes were drawn to one particular spot on the balcony. Although I couldn't see her, I felt like my Oma was there, gazing lovingly down at me, just as she had so lovingly gazed up at me from her sickbed just a few days before. My heart still aches to be separated from her, but every time I go to the D.C. Temple, my eyes are still drawn to Oma's balcony, half expecting to see her smiling down. It is a tender mercy of the Lord, a reminder that He has prepared a way for us to be with our loved ones again, and that way is through His holy temple.

– D. Anderson, Washington D.C.

Seattle Washington

Announcement:	November 15, 1975
Dedication:	November 17-21, 1980 by Spencer W. Kimball
Site:	23.5 acres
Floor Area:	110,000 square feet
Exterior Finish:	White marble and cast stone

An Old Church Pamphlet

As a teenager, I attended the Seattle Washington Temple on our scheduled youth temple trips. During the past three years, I have been attending college in Provo and have enjoyed attending nearby Utah temples. Because there is a constant stream of people wanting to attend the temples in Utah, the baptistries are always open.

This summer I was visiting family and friends, in Seattle and I really wanted to make it out to the temple while I was in town for a few weeks. I asked my mom and my sister to see if there were any youth temple trips that I could join while I was there. My mom found an old pamphlet from an earlier church meeting explaining that during the summer the Seattle Temple would be having open baptistry times on certain dates, allowing members to attend without making an appointment. It was a perfect heaven-sent opportunity. As soon as we found that piece of paper, I went upstairs, changed into Sunday clothes, and left within 20 minutes of even having the idea of going to the temple. It was amazing, and I felt so much peace, which is something I'd been seeking since leaving school. I was able to attend every week that I was home in Seattle because of what we found on that church announcement. I'm so grateful that I could attend the temple in Seattle.

I love all temples because I know what they are: houses of God. But, just as for anyone else who grew up in the area, the Seattle Temple will always have a special place in my heart.

–Danielle Self, Washington

Jordan River Utah

Announcement: February 3, 1978

Dedication: November 16-20, 1981
by Marion G. Romney

Site: 15 acres

Floor Area: 148,236 square feet

Exterior Finish: Cast stone with white marble chips; tower made of cemlite

Interesting Facts

- The Jordan River Utah Temple is the highest capacity temple in the Church, with six ordinance rooms, each seating 125 patrons, and is one of the busiest temples in the world.

- At the unconventional groundbreaking ceremony of the Jordan River Utah Temple, President Spencer W. Kimball delivered his address, offered the dedicatory prayer, and then mounted a huge Caterpillar tractor – operating the controls to move a giant shovelful of dirt.

- The construction of the Jordan River Utah Temple and its maintenance costs for many years were funded entirely by monetary donations from local members. The temple site was likewise gifted to the Church.

- Just hours before the dedication of the Jordan River Utah Temple, news correspondents announced that President Spencer W. Kimball, who was recovering from surgery and a lengthy hospital stay, would likely be confined to his room at the Hotel Utah during the dedication services. But with tears of joy, he was welcomed to the celestial room just before the ceremony commenced.

JORDAN RIVER
TEMPLE

THE CHURCH OF JESUS CHRIST
OF
LATTER-DAY SAINTS

JORDAN RIVER
TEMPLE

THE CHURCH OF JESUS CHRIST
OF
LATTER-DAY SAINTS

Blessings of Protection

When my little brother told me he was going to be deployed to Afghanistan in 2013, I panicked. I immediately thought of every worst-case scenario that could possibly befall him, and my overactive imagination threatened to send me into an emotional tailspin. I felt completely helpless in my Utah suburb, knowing he would soon be halfway around the world in a hostile environment where there were people who would actually want to do him harm. I knew I could pray and fast for him, but in this case and at this particular point in my life, I felt I needed to do more. I needed to make some sort of offering of time – something that would seal my prayers and fasting while proving to the Lord that I meant what I said when I prayed and fasted for his safety.

I was dedicated to the gospel at this point in my life, but struggling with many, many questions. The thought occurred to me that I should attend the temple weekly to write my brother's name on the prayer roll, and I knew this would not only be an acceptable offering to the Lord, but that it was also a direction my life needed to take.

I arranged with a friend to swap babysitting and began attending the Jordan River Temple every single week. I was worried I wouldn't be able to fit this time slot into my life, but soon became amazed at how easy the Lord made it for me to get to the temple during this time period.

In those hushed, but busy, rooms of the temple, I came to understand my worth as a daughter of God. I had so many questions that I had always kept close to my heart but had been afraid to pull out and examine. As I did work for the dead, I found many answers – and the answers were greater than I could have imagined. I sometimes felt as if my brain had been opened up and knowledge poured inside. Gradually – oh, so gradually – my fears for my brother began to evaporate and were replaced with peace. I was still concerned for his safety, but I had a sure knowledge that he was in the Lord's hands – and that knowledge buoyed me up whenever my imagination began to run wild.

He eventually returned safe and sound. I thought that was the only blessing I wanted and needed from this experience, but in that temple I learned that Heavenly Father has so much to give – and we don't even always know how much we need until we are there.

I was worried I wouldn't be able to fit this time slot into my life, but soon became amazed at how easy the Lord made it for me to get to the temple during this time period.

– *Rebecca Brown Wright, Utah*

ATLANTA TEMPLE
THE CHURCH OF JESUS CHRIST
OF
LATTER-DAY SAINTS

Atlanta Georgia

Announcement: April 2, 1980

Dedication: June 1-4, 1983
by Gordon B. Hinckley

Rededication: May 1, 2011

Site: 9.6 acres

Floor Area: 34,500 square feet

Exterior Finish: Precast stone

Interesting Facts

- The Atlanta Georgia Temple was the first temple dedicated by President Gordon B. Hinckley.

- The originally proposed design for the Atlanta Georgia Temple fell short of "Mormon Temple" status in the eyes of a Faith & Values reviewer for the *Atlanta Journal-Constitution*, who noted the absence of a spire and gold angel. Church Public Affairs Director for Atlanta, Donald Conkey, forwarded the review to the First Presidency. A short time later, on January 10, 1982, Church architect Emil B. Fetzer announced revised plans for the temple, which commenced a tradition of including a spire and angel Moroni on every successive Latter-day Saint temple.

- Beginning in July 2009, the Atlanta Georgia Temple underwent extensive remodeling and renovation. The crystal from the original celestial room chandelier was crushed and incorporated into the art glass windows of the remodeled celestial room. Marble from the original altars was laid into the pulpit of the chapel.

Cherished Memories

I remember as a child, I would walk around temple grounds with my family. It didn't matter whether we were walking on temple grounds in Los Angeles, Washington D.C., or Orlando, Florida – I would always feel peace. I know this peace comes from God and that the temple is a house of God. I love going to the temple. A temple is a place where families can be sealed together for time and all eternity.

I was married and sealed in the Atlanta Georgia Temple to my wonderful husband, Adam, on December 17, 2002. Since then we have attended the temple with many family members and friends in many other states. However, the Atlanta Temple will hold a dear place in

The Atlanta Temple will hold a dear place in our hearts because of the experiences we had there.

our hearts because of the experiences that we had there. My husband and I both received our endowments there at different times prior to our missions. We went to an endowment session before our temple sealing with both sets of parents. I felt the love of the Lord and our parents as we sat near each other learning about the plan of our Heavenly Father and our role in it. I will never forget how I saw my dear father and father-in-law with tears in their eyes as we sat in the sealing room that day.

I know the temple is a place where we can learn more about God's plan, feel peace from life's stresses and distractions, and receive answers to life's questions.

– Bernadene A. Carter, North Carolina

Boise Idaho

Announcement: March 31, 1982

Dedication: May 25-30, 1984
by Gordon B. Hinckley

Rededication: November 18, 2012

Site: 4.83 acres

Floor Area: 35,868 square feet

Exterior Finish: White granite

Interesting Facts

- The Boise Idaho Temple was dedicated in 24 sessions – more dedicatory sessions than had been held for any temple since the Salt Lake Temple.

- About 70,000 visitors were expected to tour the Boise Idaho Temple during its 19-day open house, but expectations were exceeded when 128,716 people toured the building. The usual number of convert baptisms more than doubled the month following the open house; people even called the mission office asking how to get baptized.

- The Boise Idaho Temple is a sister building to the Dallas Texas Temple and the Chicago Illinois Temple.

Coming Home

As a youth I took part in going to the Los Angeles Temple to do baptisms for the dead. I took that for granted. During my 21 years of being inactive in the Church, I looked at the temple from the outside only and thought that was how it would be for the rest of my life. My husband had become a member of The Church of Jesus Christ of Latter-day Saints in June 2011, after receiving a blessing that saved his life, but I was still inactive.

In 2012 we were living in Boise, Idaho, and my husband, Chuck, and I toured the Boise Idaho Temple before it was rededicated. As we walked into the sealing room, tears filled Chuck's eyes, and the hair on my arms rose. I knew it was in the cards for me to go through the temple for myself.

We ended up moving to Columbia, South Carolina, due to work. I returned to church, and my husband and I even served as Sunbeam teachers to five young boys. It took some time, but on February 22, 2014, my husband and I received our endowments in the Columbia South Carolina Temple.

We knew we wanted to be sealed in that very special room in the Boise Temple, so on May 31, 2014, with family and friends, we went to the Boise Temple to be sealed. My heart was full, and the love I feel from other members of the Church helps me know I am where I belong.

I am living proof that the love of Jesus Christ and our Heavenly Father is real and even after years of being away from the true Church, I am truly blessed and I am now prepared for my eternal life.

– Sharron Clevenstine, Washington

Dallas Texas

Announcement:	July 28, 1847
Dedication:	April 6-24, 1893 by Wilford Wooduff
Site:	10 acres
Floor Area:	253,000 square feet
Exterior Finish:	Quartz monzonite quarried from Little Cottonwood Canyon

A Complete Family

It was October of 1996 when I first got the prompting at the Dallas Temple to have another baby. My husband was working and going to school full-time, trying to get into physician assistant school. We were barely making it financially, and adding another baby into the equation would mean more expenses. I just did not see any way we would be able to afford having more children.

I ignored the prompting, thinking Heavenly Father would understand that we simply could not afford to have another baby. The Dallas Temple was six hours away from where we lived, and with my husband's work and school schedule, we only had the opportunity to attend once a month. As we attended the temple the following month, I had the same exact prompting. This time I was even more convinced we could not afford to have another baby. We were waiting to hear from any of the physician assistant schools to which my husband had applied. My husband made it clear that we had to wait until after he was done with PA school.

I didn't tell my husband about the second prompting, knowing that it would only add more stress to him as a provider. As we went home the prompting was all I could think about. Weeks passed, and I felt all the more convinced that we had to have faith and do what we were told.

December came, and we prepared for our monthly temple trip. That month was special because we were able to go as a couple, instead of taking turns attending sessions, because we had a family member watch the kids. I entered the celestial room, still feeling an undeniable prompting.

As we went home the prompting was all I could think about. Weeks passed and I felt all the more convinced that we had to have faith and do what we were told.

The Spirit was so strong that as I sat to say a prayer, not only could I feel my unborn son's presence, but it was as if I could actually hear him saying, "Mom, I'm ready to come down." As I sat there with tears in my eyes, I turned to face my husband. He knew what I was going to say. This time we obeyed the prompting. Ten days later my husband got accepted to a physician assistant school. Our third boy, Jaron, was born in November of the following year.

– Benjeline Misalucha Quirante, Texas

DALLAS TEMPLE
THE CHURCH OF JESUS CHRIST OF LATTER-DAY SAINTS

Chicago Illinois

Announcement: April 1, 1981

Dedication: August 9-13, 1985
by Gordon B. Hinckley

Rededication: October 8, 1989

Site: 13 acres

Floor Area: 34,00 square feet

Exterior Finish: Gray marble and slate roof

Interesting Facts

- The Chicago Illinois Temple closed on September 3, 1988, for remodeling that more than doubled its size.

- On Christmas Eve of 2008, a frozen ceiling sprinkler pipe burst inside the temple, causing extensive water damage. An army of craftsmen from as far away as New Mexico replaced all of the carpet, replaced over 2,000 feet of wood trim, and replaced or reupholstered most of the furniture in just two months.

Excerpt from Dedicatory Prayer

We are met in Thy holy house, erected on the soil of Illinois, to dedicate unto Thee Thy temple. One hundred and thirty-nine years ago our forebears fled this area, leaving behind the temple that they had just constructed. As they moved west across the Iowa prairie their last lingering look was at the tower of that holy edifice which had come with tremendous cost and out of unwavering faith and devotion.

On this day, in this new and beautiful Chicago temple, we of this generation remember Nauvoo. We think of the sacred edifice that stood high on its hill. We remember with appreciation and gratitude those who built it. We recall their sacrifice when they were driven from it. Knowing they soon would be banished, and with many of their number already gone, they yet chose to complete it and dedicate it unto Thee.

O God, we thank Thee for the inheritance of faith that has come down from that generation. We thank Thee for a new and better day when our people have returned to this area, and large numbers have been added to Thy Church in this part of the nation.

We are reminded also that Thy first house built in this dispensation was constructed at Kirtland, Ohio. When that sacred edifice was dedicated Thy prophet, Joseph Smith, received through revelation from Thee the dedicatory prayer which included this plea:

"Remember all Thy Church, O Lord, with all their families…that the kingdom, which Thou hast set up without hands, may become a great mountain and fill the whole earth;

"That Thy Church may come forth out of the wilderness of darkness, and shine forth fair as the moon, clear as the sun, and terrible as an army with banners;

"And be adorned as a bride for that day when Thou shalt unveil the heavens…that Thy glory may fill the earth."

Heavenly Father, we see the dawning of that glorious day. The morning breaks, and the sunlight of truth is spreading over the earth.

Heavenly Father, we see the dawning of that glorious day. The morning breaks, and the sunlight of truth is spreading over the earth. Thy people, once few in number, have become a great multitude, living in many lands and speaking many tongues. Their numbers are constantly increasing. The virtue of their lives is widely acclaimed. We are profoundly grateful for Thy blessings upon Thy work and upon Thy faithful Saints across the earth…

May this holy house, built in peace and dedicated in faith, stand as a testimony that the oppression of the past has faded and that Thy people today enjoy the precious blessings of worshipping Thee according to Thy revelations without fear or molestation. May Thy work move forward to the encompassing glory Thou hast set for it, we humbly pray, as in faith we rededicate ourselves to Thy service, with songs of thanksgiving and praise, in the name of Thy Beloved Son, the Prince of Life, our gracious and generous Redeemer, the Lord Jesus Christ. Amen.

– Gordon B. Hinckley

Denver Colorado

Announcement: March 31, 1982

Dedication: October 24-28, 1986
by Ezra Taft Benson

Site: 7.5 acres

Floor Area: 29,117 square feet

Exterior Finish: Stone

Interesting Facts

- In an act of hope and faith, one Denver-area stake started a temple fund years before the Denver Colorado Temple was announced. They gathered enough donations to pay for the assessment for the construction of the temple far ahead of time.

- Neighbors initially rejected the proposed nightly floodlighting of the Denver Colorado Temple. So, Church officials agreed to turn off the lights by 11:00 PM. In time, however, the neighbors came to appreciate the singular beauty of the temple and asked that the lights remain on all night.

One Step Closer to Eternity

One of my wife's first visits to the Denver Temple was the day we were married for time and all eternity. We had dated for almost a year, and we were ready to take the next step in our lives to becoming an eternal family.

The morning of May 4, 2013, was still cool, but the sun was shining brightly. Surrounded by family and friends, she made her way from her hotel room, and I made my way from my parents' house toward our destination: the Denver Temple. There we were, one step closer to eternity.

We showed our temple recommends to the white-haired man at the entrance, testifying in a small way of our dedication to living the gospel of Jesus Christ. Even though we were imperfect people, it was our aim to become more like Him and our Father.

But things would not be so easy. We had forgotten a document that was a nine-hour drive away. We waited anxiously in the temple recorder's

Even though we were imperfect people, it was our aim of becoming more like Him and our Father. But things would not be so easy.

office, searching for a solution that we were worried would not be found. We prayed together for almost an hour, asking Heaven for a way to be created so that we could be sealed that day. We had done all we could to prepare for marriage up to that point, and we trusted that God would provide a way. And He did!

Ten minutes later, we walked hand-in-hand into a room that was bursting with love and radiated happiness from friends and family. I couldn't help but smile, and neither could Alissa. They were true smiles. These smiles came from our hearts. We knelt down and listened to the counsel and the words of the sealing ordinance. All of the anxiety, discomfort, and struggle we felt during the previous hour had melted away, revealing pure joy.

We'll never forget the joy all of us in that room felt that day. The temple brought us all together – one step closer to eternity.

— *James Voss, Colorado*

Portland Oregon

Announcement:	April 7, 1984
Dedication:	August 19-21, 1989 by Gordon B. Hinckley
Site:	7.3 acres
Floor Area:	80,500 square feet
Exterior Finish:	White marble

Interesting Facts

- The Portland Oregon Temple sits on land originally purchased in the 1960s for a Church junior college. Later, when that decision was reversed, 7.3 acres were retained for the temple.

- A whopping 314,232 visitors toured the Portland Oregon Temple during its public open house. At the time, this was the fifth-highest number of temple open house visitors in Church history.

HOLINESS TO THE
LORD
THE HOUSE OF THE
LORD

THE CHURCH OF
JESUS CHRIST
OF LATTER-DAY
SAINTS

Las Vegas Nevada

Announcement: April 7, 1984

Dedication: December 16-18, 1989
by Gordon B. Hinckley

Site: 10.3 acres

Floor Area: 80,350 square feet

Exterior Finish: Precast stone walls with copper roof

She Was with Us

In early 2008, my grandma, Verla Jenson, was deteriorating from brain cancer, and at the same time my family was preparing for my brother to be married. She was bedridden, and her frustration was evident in the many conversations we had about attending the temple when my brother's soon-to-be wife received her endowments, as well as later for the sealing. She just could not understand why she wouldn't be allowed to get out of that bed and go with us.

June 7, the day of the endowment, rolled around and we headed to the Las Vegas Nevada Temple. I thought of my grandma as I sat peacefully in the beautiful celestial room and wished she could be with us.

It wasn't long after we left the temple that we received the phone call informing us she had passed away. I believe wholeheartedly that she was there at the temple with us after all.

– Shelbee Ropte, Iowa

Interesting Facts

- Following the announcement of the Las Vegas Nevada Temple, members of the temple district were asked to contribute toward construction. They enthusiastically answered the call, raising $11 million – 428 percent of their assessment.
- During the 23-day open house of the Las Vegas Nevada Temple, 297,480 visitors toured the edifice. More than 99,000 visited the missionary pavilion following their tour, and missionaries reported that teaching appointments tripled in the valley as a result of the temple's opening.

San Diego California

Announcement:	April 7, 1984
Dedication:	April 25-30, 1993 by Gordon B. Hinckley
Site:	7.2 acres
Floor Area:	72,000 square feet
Exterior Finish:	Marble and plaster

Interesting Facts

- After suffering a mild heart attack four months earlier, President Ezra Taft Benson made his first trip outside the Salt Lake Valley to break ground for the San Diego California Temple – his first time presiding over a temple groundbreaking.

- On Monday, December 23, 1991, the 186th anniversary of the birth of the Prophet Joseph Smith, a gilded statue of the angel Moroni was installed atop the eastern spire of the San Diego California Temple. Shortly after the setting, a traveling flock of seagulls – a bird of symbolic significance to the Church – circled the new statue about three times before continuing on its course.

- President Benson's ailing health did not allow him to preside at the dedication of the San Diego California Temple. President Gordon B. Hinckley, his first counselor, was assigned to dedicate the temple in 23 sessions.

Unique Architecture, Inside and Out

The San Diego Temple is not only recognized by many architects as one of the unique buildings of the world, but it is also the only temple in the Church to be designed, both inside and out, by a non-LDS architect and a non-LDS designer who met, fell in love while building the temple, and were married. Dennis Hyndman, project architect, and Shelly Hyndman, interior design architect, are Roman Catholic. Interestingly, the building of the temple ran into such high cost overruns that the original design material for the exterior of the temple, white marble, had to be changed to marble chips in plaster.

Additionally, due to the cost overruns, President Hinckley made the decision to not put in the previously planned visitors' center.

The temple has as its overall motif the eight-pointed star and it is found throughout the interior and exterior of the temple. The San Diego Temple is also the second-most popular temple in the Church for temple marriages and sealings. It is where both our children were married, each in one of the two larger "gold rooms," designated by the eight-pointed star in the ceiling above the chandelier in either silver or gold.

– Richard Doutre'Jones, Utah

There Will Your Heart Be Also

Having grown up in San Diego and attending the temple there, I realized a temple is a nexus – a connecting point between heaven and earth. Its purpose is to lift mankind upward to the divine, helping them come closer to God. It offers a communion experience of introspection, education, and revelation.

Nephi recorded that he "did go into the mount oft" to pray and be shown "great things" (1 Nephi 18:3). In our day, dedicated temples have replaced primitive mountain experiences yet offer the same opportunities and outcomes.

We are invited – and expected – to periodically pause our lives in the valley below to hike up the mountain and seek God's face. Jesus taught that our treasure is where our heart is (Luke 12:34), but sometimes it also matters where our physical body is. Let's treasure the temple by spending more time there.

– Connor Boyack, California

> *We are invited – and expected – to periodically pause our lives in the valley below to hike up the mountain and seek God's face.*

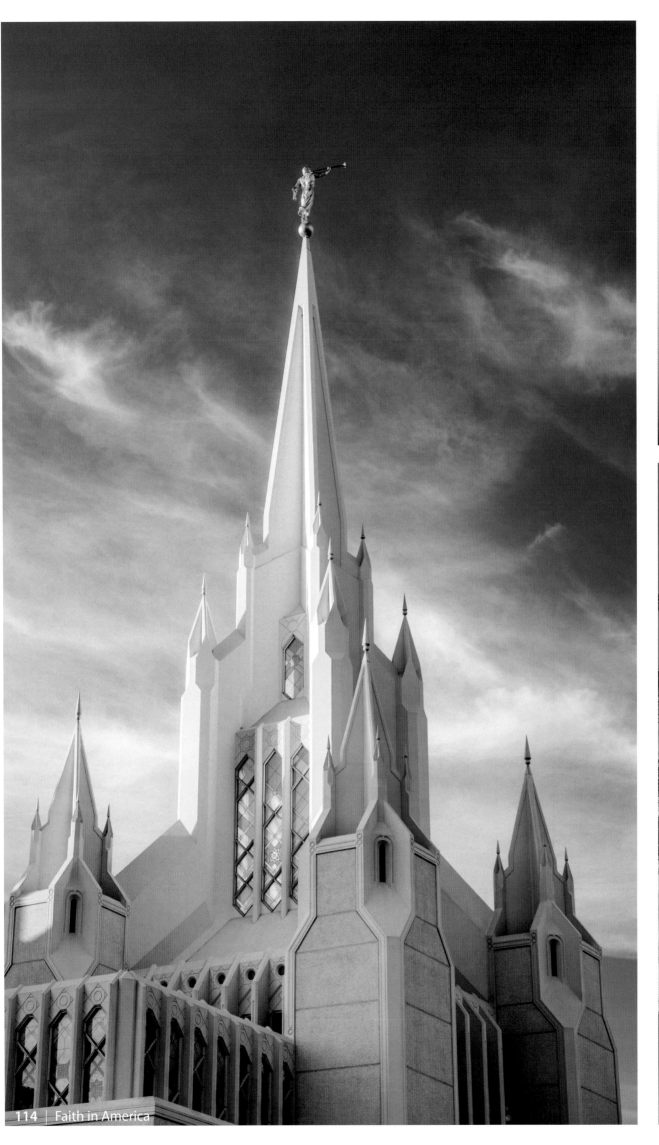

THE HOUSE OF THE LORD · HOLINESS TO THE LORD
THE CHURCH OF JESUS CHRIST OF LATTER-DAY SAINTS

Orlando Florida

Announcement:	February 17, 1990
Dedication:	October 9-11, 1994 by Howard W. Hunter
Site:	13 acres
Floor Area:	70,000 square feet
Exterior Finish:	Precast concrete and marble

My First Temple

The Orlando Florida Temple holds a special place in my heart. As a youth, it was my closest temple, and I traveled two hours one way to get to it. Doing baptisms always brought the Spirit and was a sacred and fun experience for me. As I grew older and my family moved to a different state, and as I myself lived in various other states, I felt that none could compare to the Orlando Temple.

I hadn't been to that temple since I was a youth, until a year and a half ago when my (now) husband and I went to be sealed. It was a sweet experience to tie my present to my future as I went from one family to starting my own. That temple will always hold a special place in my heart.

I have grown not only to love the beauty of the temple, but also to love the feelings I have while I'm there. I have a testimony of temples, which started and changed my life forever with the Orlando Temple. While this specific one is special to me, I know that all the temples bring the blessings of happiness and peace to our lives. I hope someday I can bring my children back to the Orlando Temple to share the blessings that have come to me.

While this specific one is special to me, I know that all the temples bring the blessings of happiness and peace to our lives.

— *Kristin Garvin, North Carolina*

To all who look upon it, including those who reside in this area, may it ever present a picture of peace and beauty, a structure partaking of Thy divine nature.

– Howard W. Hunter

Bountiful Utah

Announcement:	February 2, 1990
Dedication:	January 8-14, 1995 by Howard W. Hunter
Site:	9 acres
Floor Area:	104,000 square feet
Exterior Finish:	White granite

Let's Do It Again!

When I was four or five years old, the Bountiful Utah Temple was announced. I remember my parents being very excited. When we visited the construction site, I remember thinking how large it was and that it was only a bunch of dirt. When I was about to turn eight years old, I learned that my grandfather was called to be the first president of the Bountiful Temple as it opened. Our whole family was so excited. His job was to volunteer three years of his life with my grandma to attend the temple every day.

I had the opportunity to attend a live session of the dedication. I remember singing a beautiful song with the entire congregation at the conclusion of the meeting. It was called "The Spirit of God." My little heart was full of a special feeling, which I later learned is called the Holy Ghost. When they finished the last note there was silence, and then a little voice shouted out, "LET'S DO IT AGAIN!" There was a chuckle as those in the room heard the little boy shout. The little boy was me. I love the Bountiful Temple!

– Ben Toney, Utah

Interesting Facts

- At the 28 dedicatory sessions of the Bountiful Utah Temple, 201,655 members were in attendance – the largest number of attendees at a temple dedication in the history of the Church.
- The floor plan created for the Bountiful Utah Temple was adapted and used for the Mount Timpanogos Utah Temple.

A Lifetime Temple

I was nine years old when I attended the dedication of the Bountiful Utah Temple. Being so young, I don't remember much about what was said that evening. I remember my parents picking me up from my friend's birthday party early to go to the dedication. I remember getting all dressed up, my hair still wet from the luau party, a white handkerchief carefully folded in my purse.

I remember the feeling I had when I listened to President Howard W. Hunter speak. All of my young girl thoughts about missing out on presents and cake quickly faded, and a quiet, comforting peace settled into my heart. I was grateful to be a part of something so special and sacred. I remember sitting next to my parents and feeling at home. From that moment on, I felt the Bountiful Temple was "my" temple.

It was on the grounds of the Bountiful temple where I received a phone call from my sister about expecting her first baby. It's where I decided to pursue a career, and then later, to set that career aside for the man I chose to marry. It's where I spent hours in the waiting room, the baptismal font, the grounds, and the atrium, fervently praying about that man I chose, and whether I was making a good decision. It's where my bishop at the time told me he felt I had made the right choice. It's where my sister and I went to be baptized and confirmed for my deceased great-grandmother, a choice experience I will never forget. The day I went through the Bountiful Temple to receive my own endowment, my mother presented me with a temple bag with the Bountiful Temple embroidered on the face. I treasure that little bag and the memories it still brings from that special day.

All of my young girl thoughts about missing out on presents and cake quickly faded, and a quiet, comforting peace settled into my heart.

I was married in the Bountiful Temple in December of 2005, almost a decade after I went to the temple dedication as a girl. The feelings of love and joy almost cannot be expressed as I thought about how every important decision I had made had led me, ultimately, to that holy place where "families can be together forever."

Now I live many miles from the Bountiful Temple. Every time I visit, I think back on my life as a young woman. I examine the woman I am now, and ponder on what my future still holds. I have a picture of the Bountiful Temple hanging on my family room wall. It is the temple of my childhood, where all my dreams were prayed about, sorted out, and realized.

– *Carmen Rasmusen Herbert, Utah*

Mt. Timpanogos Utah

Announcement: October 3, 1992

Dedication: October 13-19, 1996
by Gordon B. Hinckley

Site: 16.7 acres

Floor Area: 107,240 square feet

Exterior Finish: White granite, art glass
and bronze doors

Through my Window

When I was a young teenager, the Church announced that a new temple would be built in American Fork, Utah. This was exciting news to me as my family had recently purchased a home in the hills of Pleasant Grove, a town only ten minutes away from the new temple site.

My bedroom window overlooked the valley, and I would spend many hours sitting on my bed, looking out at the spot where the temple would one day stand. I pictured the day I would be married in that temple and had hopes that a beautiful, eternal family was in my future.

The temple was completed during my senior year of high school. Its open house and dedication were the first I had ever attended, and my love for the temple only grew. If I ever needed a place of peace, solitude, or prayer, the temple grounds were my retreat.

On December 24, my boyfriend took me for a drive, on the premise that we had some Christmas gifts to deliver. Instead, we ended up on the grounds of the Mount Timpanogos Temple, where he asked me to marry him. My childhood dreams came true on May 6, when we were married there. I continued to retreat to the temple for clarity, and sometimes brought my children along to walk around the grounds and feel the peace that could be felt. I distinctly remember my two-year-old daughter climbing out of the car, looking high towards the angel Moroni statue, and in a voice full of awe, exclaiming, "Mom! God!"

> *My bedroom window overlooked the valley, and I would spend many hours sitting on my bed, looking out at the spot where the temple would one day stand.*

In 2012, we were blessed to adopt our son. The journey to bring him to our family had been difficult, and the temple had been my strength during the times I had nothing left to give. He was a miracle, and the crowning moment was the day we were able to be sealed to him. As I sat in the sealing room of the Mount Timpanogos Temple with my husband and five children, I thought back to my childhood – to those moments where I looked out at the temple site and dreamed of my eternal family. The temple, and specifically the Mount Timpanogos Temple, had always been my goal, but I couldn't have comprehended the joy I would feel in the temple that day. Because of the temple, my family would be together forever.

– Rachel Whitaker Galbraith, Utah

Interesting Facts

- No location was specified when the Mount Timpanogos Utah Temple was announced in General Conference as a temple for "Utah County." The location was announced six months later, at the following Conference, as the former site of a Church welfare farm in American Fork.
- On July 17, 1995, a 13-foot-3-inch gold-leafed statue of the angel Moroni was set atop the Mount Timpanogos Utah Temple to an audience of an estimated 20,000, who clogged the surrounding streets. Once the statue was in place, the throng of visitors broke into applause and then spontaneously began to sing "The Spirit of God."

St. Louis Missouri

Announcement:	December 29, 1990
Dedication:	June 1-5, 1997 by Gordon B. Hinckley
Site:	14 acres
Floor Area:	58,749 square feet
Exterior Finish:	White granite

Interesting Facts

- During the four-week public open house of the St. alb Missouri Temple, nearly 260,000 visitors toured the building with 11,518 on the first day alone. Demand for the free tickets was so high that tours were conducted on two of the four Sundays, though it was originally planned that no tours would be held on Sundays. Reaction was overwhelmingly positive with visitors demonstrating genuine interest and curiosity.

- Construction of the St. Louis Missouri Temple was well received by residents and enthusiastically welcomed by the mayor, aldermen, and alderwoman of Town and Country and other local officials. Their warm reception reflected the refuge found in St. Louis in the 1830s when Saints fled from persecution in Western Missouri and Illinois.

Spiritual Fire

Waiting to move to Portland, Oregon, to join my husband, who had secured a new job, my children and I stayed behind so my oldest boy could graduate from high school. Our home sold very quickly so we moved to a furnished apartment, and I found myself with a lot of time on my hands. Our stake was the home stake of the newly finished St. Louis Temple, and there I found a good place to use my time.

On Saturday night, before the first dedication session, a choir from outside the area had come into the temple at eight o'clock to rehearse in the building in preparation for the session the following day. They were the last to rehearse, and it had been a long day.

As traffic was traveling by the temple that night, a driver called 911 saying the temple was on fire. A fire engine quickly made its way to the temple and checked but found no fire.

The next morning President Hinckley told us a story about this event. The choir had come to the temple under unusual circumstances. The choir director had never directed a choir and some members had never sung in a choir, but because of their obedience and sacrifice, the Spirit was strong as they rehearsed. President Hinckley told us that the Lord Jesus Christ had sanctified the temple during the presentation of their music. The flames were representative of the same fire that was observed at the Kirtland temple.

I will never forget the feelings and love I have for the St. Louis Temple.

– Elaine Barnett, California

Vernal Utah

Announcement:	February 13, 1994
Dedication:	November 2-4, 1997 by Gordon B. Hinckley
Site:	1.6 acres
Floor Area:	38,771 square feet
Exterior Finish:	Brick

Interesting Facts

- The Vernal Utah Temple was the first temple built from an existing building – the Uintah Stake Tabernacle.

- At the dedication of the Uintah Stake Tabernacle on August 24, 1907, President Joseph F. Smith's words would prove prophetic when he said he "would not be surprised if the day would come when a temple would be built in your own midst here."

- The Vernal Utah Temple is labeled 1907 and 1997, indicating the two years when the building was dedicated – first as a tabernacle and then as a temple.

- The idea of converting the Uintah Stake Tabernacle into the Vernal Utah Temple was first proposed by leaders of the Vernal Utah Glines Stake to area authorities in 1984, but the proposal was eventually rejected. Many other possibilities were pursued, and the building had even been put up for sale for a time. However, in 1993, the idea of a temple was proposed again. This time, it met with First Presidency approval.

- The Reader Home, a turn-of-the-century residence in Vernal, became the source of thousands of needed replacement bricks for the Vernal Utah Temple. The owner, a friend of another faith who planned to raze the home, agreed to donate it to the Church instead. For two months, 16,000 bricks were painstakingly removed from the home and brought to the temple.

Touch the hearts of Thy people with a great desire to come here frequently and serve in a singular work of dedication.

-Gordon B. Hinckley

Monticello Utah

Announcement: October 4, 1997

Dedication: November 17, 2002
by Gordon B. Hinckley

Site: 1.33 acres

Floor Area: 11,225 square feet

Exterior Finish: Off-white marble from Turkey

The Organist

The Monticello Temple was the first of the smaller sized temples, and seats in the celestial room dedication were at a premium, reserved first for general authorities, stake presidency members, bishops and their families, and I did not fit into any of those categories. So I began to look for other ways to be in the celestial room with our prophet, President Hinckley. I knew the choir was able to enter the celestial room, but I was not the best alto in the stake. Such was my frame of mind when a member of the stake high council knocked on my door early on a Sunday morning in March and asked if I would play the organ at our stake's dedication session. In my excitement, I did not let the fact that I don't know how to play the organ keep me from saying YES!! You see, I knew that the organist was seated in the celestial room. This was my ticket in, and though I was not an organist, I had four months to become one.

To my credit, I did know how to play the piano, although marginally. And so began the most intensive, focused, stressful four months of organ study in Church history, I'm sure. I practiced every free moment until I learned to play the most challenging of songs. I learned about stops, the great and the swell, drawknobs and pedals. It was hard, and many times I wondered what I had done thinking I could pull this off. I worked, prayed, received priesthood blessings, and by dedication day, I was prepared and ready for one of the most incredible experiences of my life. I sat so close to a prophet of God I could have reached out and touched him. I was so awestruck when he announced me as the organist that I forgot to pull out the third page of a three-page song and had nowhere to go at the end of the second page of music. It was a perfect day, simply a little moment of heaven on earth, and I often wonder if I am working as hard for an eternity in the celestial kingdom as I did for a few hours in the celestial room of the Monticello Temple.

— Carri Cozzens, Utah

Anchorage Alaska

Announcement:	October 4, 1997
Dedication:	January 9-10, 1999 by Gordon B. Hinckley
Rededication:	February 8, 2004
Site:	5.4 acres
Floor Area:	11,937 square feet
Exterior Finish:	Sierra white granite

The Privilege of Proximity

Most of the kids I taught in seminary had been to the temple for the dedication, for the rededication, and to perform ordinances. The temple was very small initially, but it was remodeled to add 3,000 square feet. Many of my seminary students met President Hinckley at the dedication and saw him again at the rededication.

Because Alaska is so large and doesn't have a lot of people per square mile, my family cleaned the temple often because we were so close. It always felt like a privilege. I was also privileged to house people who traveled long distances to go to the temple, again because we were so close.

It felt peaceful being among the beauty and the peace of the temple.

The temple was small, and it had a small population that it was serving. So often when I called to make a reservation I could tell who was answering the phone by their voice. I really loved that. It was easy to know and love everyone there.

It was wonderful to see the temple every day, as a reminder that I needed to be there. The Anchorage Temple was a blessing to the people in Alaska because prior to its construction, the distance to other temples made it difficult to attend; people had to fly to Seattle or drive to Calgary. That is why the "small" temples were such a blessing. Everyone in the Church felt lucky to have a temple in our midst.

Everyone in the Church felt lucky to have a temple in our midst.

– *Kaylene Myres Coleman, Texas*

Interesting Facts

- The Anchorage Alaska Temple is the northernmost temple of the Church.
- The floors of the temple are heated because it is so cold.
- The 700-pound Celestial Room chandelier of the Anchorage Alaska Temple features thousands of Hungarian crystals and 140 lights that make the room's windows appear gold from the outside.
- On, Thursday, March 22, 2007, an accidental fire erupted in the 30-year-old stake center adjacent to the Anchorage Alaska Temple, destroying most of the roof and causing extension damage; it was rebuilt over the next year. The following day, a water line burst in the temple basement, flooding it with 3–5 feet of water; the building was shortly restored to working order.

Spokane
Washington

Announcement:	August 13, 1988
Dedication:	August 21-23, 1999 by Gordon B. Hinckley
Site:	2 acres
Floor Area:	10,700 square feet
Exterior Finish:	Granite

Interesting Facts

- In March 2009, nearly a decade after its dedication, the Spokane Washington Temple received a new angel Moroni statue atop its spire. Instead of facing east as the original statue did, it was positioned facing west – the same orientation as the temple.

- On August 22, 2009, in commemoration of the 10th anniversary of the dedication of the Spokane Washington Temple, members of the Spokane Washington East Stake ensured that every seat in every session was filled the entire day.

Columbus Ohio

Announcement:	April 25, 1998
Dedication:	September 4-5 1999 by Gordon B. Hinckley
Site:	1.35 acres
Floor Area:	10,700 square feet
Exterior Finish:	Imperial white marble

Interesting Facts

- The Columbus Ohio Temple is located 150 miles south of Kirtland, Ohio, where the restored Church dedicated its first temple in 1836.

- The beautiful white Vermont marble facing on the exterior was quarried near Sharon, Vermont, birthplace of the Prophet Joseph Smith.

COLUMBUS OHIO TEMPLE

Bismarck
North Dakota

Announcement: July 29, 1988

Dedication: September 19 1999
by Gordon B. Hinckley

Site: 1.6 acres

Floor Area: 10,700 square feet

Exterior Finish: Granite from Quebec

Interesting Facts

- Prior to the dedication, President Gordon B. Hinckley had never been to North Dakota, the only state he had never visited. Members rejoiced to have the prophet in their midst.

- The members of the temple district are scattered over a large region, and the completion of the temple brought its blessings much closer to the Saints. Previous to its construction, those living in Grand Forks, North Dakota, had to make a 16-hour trip to attend the temple in Chicago.

Members in Minot, North Dakota, drove 14 hours to Cardston, Alberta. Saints in Rapid City, South Dakota, traveled seven hours to Denver. Robert B. Dahlgren, the Bismarck Temple's first president, noted that members of the district are highly dedicated and used to traveling long distances. He spoke of a retired couple who lived some distance from Bismarck who readily agreed to move to Bismarck to work in the temple full-time.[3]

Columbia
South Carolina

Announcement:	September 11, 1988
Dedication:	October 16-17, 1999 by Gordon B. Hinckley
Site:	3.6 acres
Floor Area:	10,700 square feet
Exterior Finish:	White marble

Excerpt from the Dedicatory Prayer

Many have yearned for this day when a temple would be built in their midst. May they now use it for the purposes for which it has been constructed.

We rejoice in the presence of this house in this great state of South Carolina that has hosted Thy messengers of eternal truth. They have been coming here for generations, and there has been established a great body of faithful Latter-day Saints. We pray that the very presence of this Thy house will have a sanctifying influence upon the people of this area, and particularly upon those who enter its portals…

Dear Father, we are so deeply grateful unto Thee for every gift Thou hast bestowed upon us. May we walk worthily before Thee at all times and in all circumstances. May Thy work grow and prosper exceedingly in this part of the earth. May faith increase in the hearts of the people. We ask it humbly, together with every other blessing that Thou seest fit to bestow upon us, and do it all as Thy sons and daughters, recognizing Thee as Our Father, in the name of Thy Divine Son, even the Lord Jesus Christ, amen.

– Gordon B. Hinckley

Detroit Michigan

Announcement:	August 10, 1998
Dedication:	October 23-24, 1999 by Gordon B. Hinckley
Site:	6.34 acres
Floor Area:	10,700 square feet
Exterior Finish:	White marble

Interesting Facts

- During the days of dedication, President Hinckley spoke with the *Church News* of the members of the Detroit Michigan Temple district: "They appreciate it very much. They have indicated that they're so deeply grateful for this sacred structure and we, too, are happy that it has been erected here and dedicated and that the work of the Lord now goes forward here in this part of the earth."
- Stephen Mack, a brother of Joseph Smith's mother, Lucy, "surveyed the first road through what became Detroit." Members point out the road in front of the temple as the one Stephen Mack built. The Prophet Joseph Smith, his brother Hyrum, and his father, Joseph Smith, Sr., visited the Detroit area in 1834.

- President Bithell, who was in charge of finding a temple site in Detroit, explained that he considered property behind the stake center, but it wasn't selected because the temple would be hidden behind the meetinghouse, and property to the north of the stake center was assumed to be too small. But after considering several properties near other meetinghouses, Pres. Bithell again looked at the tree-covered lot outside his office window and wondered about the northward property. It was measured "and it was just perfect," he said. He said the lot was part of the original eight acres purchased for Michigan's first stake center in 1952. Although selling the piece was often under consideration, it never happened.[4]

Billings Montana

Announcement:	August 30, 1996
Dedication:	November 20–21, 1999 by Gordon B. Hinckley
Site:	10 acres
Floor Area:	33,800 square feet
Exterior Finish:	White dolomite concrete

Preserved for Dedication

Sister Rose Griffin Doty of Byron, Wyoming, felt her life was preserved so she could attend the dedication of the Billings Montana Temple. Sister Doty was born in Burlington, Wyoming, about the time Mormon colonists were sent to the Bighorn Basin. Due to her ailing health earlier in the fall, her family arranged a special trip for her to see the nearly completed temple several weeks before the dedication. However, she said she was strengthened to be able to attend the dedication, in part because she wanted to see President Hinckley, with whom she had a special experience. After her husband, Joseph Doty, passed away, she labored in the Southern States Mission in the early 1960s and was set apart by President Hinckley. "I have always admired him for his support for me when I was on my mission. I wanted to thank him for a temple and for the prayer he said when he set me apart, which I have always remembered," she said.

Sister Doty is among the many who had faithfully served at the Idaho Falls Idaho Temple in the past. For many in Montana and Wyoming, the drive to Idaho Falls took from up to six hours in the summer when they could cut through Yellowstone Park, to eight or more hours in the winter when the more direct route was closed. Those Saints are grateful that several hours will be cut from the travel time to attend the temple.[5]

Interesting Facts

- About 4,800 people gathered during a spring snowstorm to witness the groundbreaking of the Billings Montana Temple. During the groundbreaking, a choir of 700 youth sang.

Raleigh
North Carolina

Announcement:	September 3, 1988
Dedication:	December 18-19, 1999 by Gordon B. Hinckley
Site:	12 acres
Floor Area:	10,700 square feet
Exterior Finish:	White marble

From the *Church News*

Though [Brother Gary Stansbury] is from Kansas City, Missouri, right next to Independence, "somehow the Church eluded me for 44 years," he said. Originally assigned to supervise a large retail project in St. Louis, Brother Stansbury was reassigned to the LDS temple in North Carolina due to a delay in St. Louis. The temple project was to be a temporary assignment, so he began to look for other work early on. However, by the time he received a substantial offer from an Atlanta company, he told them to call back in December. The building was completed in a record six months. "I had to stay and build this temple," he said. "I needed to be here. And thinking back now, it almost seems that I've kind of been led to learn for 44 years, and now, this [joining the Church] is what I'm supposed to do."[6]

Interesting Facts

- The Raleigh North Carolina Temple's timely dedication in December 1999 was indeed a fitting offering to the Lord while the world observed His birth of nearly 2,000 years before.
- The temple was dedicated just five days before the 194th anniversary of the birth of Joseph Smith, prophet of the Restoration. For North Carolina Latter-day Saints whose legacy extends back to the days when Jedediah M. Grant first preached the gospel there in 1838, the temple was a welcome gift, as well.

RALEIGH NORTH CAROLINA TEMPLE
THE CHURCH OF JESUS CHRIST OF LATTER-DAY SAINTS

St. Paul Minnesota

Announcement:	July 29, 1998
Dedication:	January 9, 2000 by Gordon B. Hinckley
Site:	7.5 acres
Floor Area:	10,700 square feet
Exterior Finish:	Granite

The Lord Chose This Place

Elder Thomas A. Holt, Area Authority Seventy and a St. Paul resident, [offered] some insight on the Church's history in the [St. Paul] area. "We've waited a long time," he said, indicating that the first known Latter-day Saints in Minnesota came in 1847 "from Nauvoo to visit their sons and were persuaded to stay." As Minnesotans were converted, the new members would move to Utah until priesthood leaders declared that members should stay where they were and build the Church. "For decades," Elder Holt continued, "the closest temple was Salt Lake City, a two-day drive."

Currently, Minnesota is in the Chicago Illinois Temple District, a seven- to fourteen-hour drive for most Minnesota members. The first stake in Minnesota was organized in 1960. "Now we have six stakes," Elder Holt said. Before the second stake was organized, he was assigned to find a site for the stake center and had "looked at several sites and felt nothing" until he came to "this beautiful site heavily wooded with oak trees." The Spirit bore witness to him that this was to be the place for the St. Paul Minnesota Stake Center, "and now the site for our Minnesota Temple. The Lord chose this place," Elder Holt said.[7]

Kona Hawaii

Announcement:	May 7, 1988
Dedication:	January 23-24, 2000 by Gordon B. Hinckley
Site:	7.02 acres
Floor Area:	10,700 square feet
Exterior Finish:	White marble

Excerpt from the Dedicatory Prayer

We pray for the well being of the faithful Saints in these beautiful isles of the Pacific. For many years now a sacred House of the Lord has stood in Laie on the island of Oahu. Saints from all over Hawaii have traveled to that house to receive those blessings which are granted only in temples of the Lord. Now we have this second temple, here on the big island. May the work increase. May there come into the hearts of the people a growing desire to come to the House of the Lord, here to taste the sweet refreshment of the Holy Spirit. May the influence of this Thy house be felt among Thy people, and may it find expression in their lives and in their homes.

We pray that the youth of the Church may have a desire to serve the needs of those beyond the veil of death through vicarious baptisms in their behalf. As they do so, may there grow in their hearts a compelling desire to walk as Thou wouldst have them walk, and not after the ways of the world.

Give them peace and joy in their hearts as they walk in faithfulness before Thee. Smile down upon them and favor them…

We ask that Thou wilt open the windows of heaven and shower down blessings upon the faithful tithe payers of the Church wherever they may be found. It is they who have made possible this sacred structure. Prosper them in their affairs. Give them peace and joy in their hearts as they walk in faithfulness before Thee. Smile down upon them and favor them with Thine encompassing love.

We pray that Thy work may strengthen throughout these islands. Bless those who serve here as missionaries and those who go from here throughout the earth as representatives of Thee and of Thy work. Endow them with a special power, that they may stand before the world and bear testimony of the divinity of Thy Beloved Son and of Thy great plan of happiness for Thy children of all generations.

— *Gordon B. Hinckley*

Albuquerque New Mexico

Announcement:	April 4, 1997
Dedication:	March 5, 2000 by Gordon B. Hinckley
Site:	8.5 acres
Floor Area:	34,245 sqaure feet
Exterior Finish:	Desert rose precast concrete trimmed with pearl granite

My Father's Last Wish

Can temples be powerful even before they are completed? Do temples have to be dedicated for their divine influence to be felt?

The answers to these questions for me began in June 1999 as my mother and five siblings gathered around my 62-year-old father's hospital bed and learned that his cancer treatment had failed. We were told that he only had a short time left in mortality. The doctors allowed him to fly back to Albuquerque, New Mexico, to spend his remaining days under hospice care in his own home. His only request was that the ambulance transporting him from the airport stop somewhere special – the Albuquerque Temple that was under construction.

My father had long hoped and prayed for this temple. He believed in the power and promises of the temple. For my dad, the temple was all about families. His own eternal family unit began after being sealed to my mother and having six children together. But his love for family also extended back generations to long-departed ancestors he had researched and come to know. He longed for a temple to be built close by, where he could regularly perform the saving ordinances for these family members. Even during his cancer treatments, he followed the groundbreaking and construction of the

> *But looking at his beaming face as he got to see his beloved Albuquerque Temple, surrounded by his family, my perspective was transformed.*

Albuquerque Temple with great interest.

As his family gathered around his ambulance stretcher, we all looked at the temple that was still months away from completion. For a moment I felt great disappointment that my father would never see "his" Albuquerque Temple dedicated. He would never stand in its holy rooms and receive precious promises on behalf of his ancestors.

But looking at his beaming face as he got to see his beloved Albuquerque Temple, surrounded by his family, my perspective was transformed. This temple may not yet have been dedicated, but the divine priesthood power it would soon contain was already present in our lives. Sacred words had already been spoken that bound him to his wife, children, parents, and family for eternity. My father passed away only 3 days later, but the promises of divine blessings and heavenly reunions remained in full force.

I am able to attend the Albuquerque Temple often now and feel the Spirit of the Lord as I worship. But that same Spirit was present 15 years before as the influence of an unfinished temple gave sweet reassurance that God's plan of happiness is true and that families really can be together forever.

– Derek Lines, New Mexico
mormonnerd.com

Louisville Kentucky

Announcement: March 17, 1999

Dedication: March 19, 2000
by Thomas S. Monson

Site: 3 acres

Floor Area: 10,700 square feet

Exterior Finish: White marble

Big or Small

Several years ago I visited Kentucky. The Louisville Temple was on the top of my list of things to see, so early one morning I packed up everything into my car and left for the Lord's house. When I got there I realized the temple was closed on this weekday. I was visiting from Germany, and the temple nearest my home was two hours away, in Switzerland, and open every day.

Not able to go inside, I spent the morning on the temple grounds, studied in my scriptures, had breakfast on the lawn, and visited the chapel next to the temple. After a while I went back to my car, opened the door and whispered: "No worries, I will be back and serve you here." It was a very cold morning and day. As I whispered to the Lord those words, the sun broke through the clouds and touched the spire of the temple.

Two days later I went back when the temple was opened. As I changed into my white clothes, I admired the beautiful rooms and enjoyed the peace. It was my very first time inside this temple. I didn't know where to go to wait for the session to start, so I asked a temple worker to direct me. She escorted me to the room, and I was surprised

> *It was a very cold morning and day. As I whispered to the Lord those words, the sun broke through the clouds and touched the spire of the temple.*

when I noticed I was waiting in the session room and not a waiting room. This temple was so small that there was no such waiting place. There were only five sisters and three brothers, and the room had only 20 seats. Although it was a small group of the Lord's servants, they had true intentions to help those who have already passed beyond the veil.

Later, in the celestial room, I said a prayer for the person I had just performed the endowment for and a prayer for myself. The Spirit of the Lord was very strong. I know that no matter how big the Lord's house is or how small the group of Saints is, the Spirit of the Lord testifies to us that this is His house.

– *Eivonny Yvonne Grimske, Germany*

Palmyra New York

Announcement: February 21, 1999

Dedication: April 6, 2000
by Gordon B. Hinckley

Site: 5 acres

Floor Area: 10,900 square feet

Exterior Finish: White granite

Interesting Facts

- The Palmyra New York Temple was the 100th announced temple of the Church.

- The site of the Palmyra New York Temple is on the east end of the original 100-acre Smith Family Farm, which is owned by the Church.

- Situated on an elevated ridge just beyond the Sacred Grove, where God the Father and Jesus Christ appeared to Joseph Smith in the spring of 1820, the Palmyra New York Temple – a House of the Lord – stands as a testimony to that singular event. Rich in Church history, the Palmyra landscape is dotted with historic sites, including the visitors' center at the foot of the Hill Cumorah, where Joseph Smith retrieved the ancient gold plates that were translated into the Book of Mormon.

- The windows in the waiting area of the Palmyra New York Temple are etched with a tree design but have been left transparent (unlike the stained glass windows that adorn the temple itself) at the request of President Gordon B. Hinckley, in order to provide a view of the Sacred Grove. An administration office was relocated during construction to further improve the view of the grove.

Thy work, begun here so humbly and with so few, has now blossomed into a vast family. Thy people are spread over the earth.

– Gordon B. Hinckley

Fresno California

Announcement:	January 8, 1999
Dedication:	April 9, 2000 by Gordon B. Hinckley
Site:	2.34 acres
Floor Area:	10,700 square feet
Exterior Finish:	White Sierra granite from Raymond, California

Aiding Souls

The Fresno Temple holds a very special place in my heart because it was the closest temple to me growing up. I was very blessed to live close to such a beautiful place. I would always look forward to going with other youth in my ward to do baptisms for the dead. As I entered the temple, I was able to leave all my worries outside and really feel the Spirit and my appreciation of the gospel. I felt like I was where I needed to be as I was performing baptisms for the dead. I always felt happy and grateful knowing I was aiding those souls in receiving the gospel.

— *Deanna Moulton, Colorado*

Medford Oregon

Announcement: March 15, 1999

Dedication: April 16, 2000
by James E. Faust

Site: 2 acres

Floor Area: 10,700 square feet

Exterior Finish: Gray granite from North Carolina

The Presence of a Grandfather

While serving as a missionary in the Eugene Oregon Mission, I had the wonderful opportunity to go to the Medford Oregon Temple. I was only in my second area and was still homesick. In the weeks leading up to this opportunity to go to the temple for the first time on my mission, my thoughts were full of my family. The temple had always been family time for us.

While my thoughts were directed on my family during the endowment session, I felt an overwhelming outpouring of love and gratitude for the sacrifice I was making as a missionary from someone present in the room with me. I looked around and beheld no one that I knew, besides my companion and a few other missionaries. Feeling that I had missed somebody, I looked again and still beheld no one. Feeling that my eyes were playing a trick on me, I decided to look again, but this time I also decided to look not only with my eyes but also with my heart. As I did that, I felt the presence of my Grandpa Shea, who had died 13 years prior. My grandpa joined the Church later in life and only had one daughter. Until that moment I had never realized that he never had a son or grandson to carry the Shea name as a missionary. While sitting in the temple that day, I felt my grandpa's love for me as a family member to bear his name as a missionary. That day I learned that while my nametag said Elder Wilkes on the outside, I also carried the nametag of Elder Shea within my heart.

– *Daniel Wilkes, Texas*

Memphis
Tennessee

Announcement: September 17, 1998

Dedication: April 23, 2000
by James E. Faust

Site: 6.35 acres

Floor Area: 10,700 square feet

Exterior Finish: Imperial white marble

Interesting Fact

- In 2003, the city of Bartlett, Tennessee, awarded the Memphis Tennessee Temple the "America in Bloom" award. The award came as a surprise to Church representatives, as they had not entered the temple in the contest. However, contest committee members can enter buildings they feel should have been considered, and such was the case with the temple.

Reno Nevada

Announcement: April 12, 1999

Dedication: April 23, 2000
by Thomas S. Monson

Site: 7.9 acres

Floor Area: 10,700 square feet

Exterior Finish: Gray granite

Interesting Facts

- The Reno Nevada Temple was dedicated in four sessions on Easter Sunday, April 23, 2000.

- Only about 200, including a 65-voice choir, were able to gather for the cornerstone ceremony, as the grounds behind the temple stop short at an iron fence before sloping steeply downward.

- President Monson waved at those in the back of the crowd, shook the hands of those in front, and warmly bantered with those assembled. Then, after having the General Authorities' wives and members of the temple presidency each take a turn at applying mortar to the cornerstone, he called for children.[8]

We pray that the divine presence of this house in this community may be felt by all who pass by, that it may be looked upon with respect and appreciation.

– Thomas S. Monson

NASHVILLE TENNESSEE TEMPLE
THE CHURCH OF JESUS CHRIST OF LATTER-DAY SAINTS

Nashville Tennessee

Announcement:	November 9, 1994
Dedication:	May 21, 2000 by James E. Faust
Site:	6.86 acres
Floor Area:	10,700 square feet
Exterior Finish:	White marble

Interesting Facts

- When the First Presidency announced plans for the Nashville Tennessee Temple, there were only four operating temples east of the Mississippi River, with a fifth under construction in St. Louis, Missouri.

- The Nashville Tennessee Temple was dedicated in four sessions on May 21, 2000, by President James E. Faust, Second Counselor in the First Presidency. Persistent cloudy skies gave way to sunshine within an hour of the first dedicatory prayer.

- The Nashville Tennessee Temple was constructed simultaneously with the Memphis Tennessee Temple, which was dedicated just a month earlier.

Baton Rouge
Louisiana

Announcement: October 14, 1998

Dedication: July 16, 2000
by Gordon B. Hinckley

Site: 6.3 acres

Floor Area: 10,700 square feet

Exterior Finish: Imperial Danby white marble from Vermont

Excerpt from the Dedicatory Prayer

We dedicate and consecrate unto Thee and to Thy Beloved Son this the Baton Rouge Louisiana Temple of The Church of Jesus Christ of Latter-day Saints.

We dedicate the ground on which it stands, that it may be holy and beautiful with the adornment of nature. We dedicate the building in its entirety, from the footings on which it rests to the figure of Moroni atop its steeple, with all of the parts and portions thereof, including the beautiful baptistry, the endowment rooms, the wonderful celestial room, the sealing rooms with their sacred altars, and all of the halls, offices, and other facilities.

May they provide a shelter of peace from the noise and clamor of the world, a refuge in time of distress, a sanctuary where Thy sons and daughters may come to commune with Thee in sacred and solemn prayer.

May no unholy hand desecrate it or defile it in any way. May no unrighteous tongue speak out against it…

Save this Thy House from the pollution of the world. May no unholy hand desecrate it or defile it in any way. May no unrighteous tongue speak out against it, but may it be looked upon by all who see it as a house that is holy unto Thee.

Protect it from the ravages of the storms that will beat upon it. Keep it ever secure and inviolate.

Wilt Thou be pleased to honor it with Thy presence, and cause Thy Holy Spirit to dwell here and touch the hearts of all who labor in these sacred precincts.

Grant unto Thy Saints a vision of the great and eternal work for which it has been constructed. May Thy people come here frequently and be refreshed by a knowledge of Thine eternal and everlasting purposes in behalf of Thy children of all generations.

– Gordon B. Hinckley

The Plan of Salvation taught in the temple with simplicity, yet with power, will be as a never-failing beacon of divine light to guide our footsteps and keep them constantly on the pathway of eternal life.

-Howard W. Hunter

Oklahoma City
Oklahoma

Announcement:	March 19, 1999
Dedication:	July 30, 2000 by James E. Faust
Site:	1 acre
Floor Area:	10,769 square feet
Exterior Finish:	White marble

From the *Church News*

A year after I was baptized into The Church of Jesus Christ of Latter-day Saints, I was called on a 30-month family history mission, beginning in September 2010. I served from home, working on my own computer at my own pace and on my own schedule. I was thrilled there was a way for me – a new convert in my 30s with a job – to still serve a mission.

During my mission, my father died of cancer. He was not a member of the LDS Church, but he loved genealogy. My mother was not a Mormon, either, but she loved indexing and had fun accumulating points for the work she did.

In January of this year, my brother and I were able to complete our father's work in the temple. It was particularly special because the youth group from my own ward was there to share the experience with us.

One week later, my mother was killed in a car accident. I do not know how I would have endured the deaths of both my parents without an eternal perspective.

Because of the strong Spirit those youth felt at the temple, they decided to accept Elder Bednar's challenge to get involved in family history work and help get the whole ward involved. Ninety-three percent of the youth participated, including less-active youth. Out of 243 households, 178 chose to be visited by the young men and young women to be taught how to do their own family history. The project culminated in a special ward temple trip to the Oklahoma City Oklahoma Temple, where we as a ward researched and brought all our own family names for each of the ordinances. We scheduled it such that our ward also provided the workers for the sessions, and many new temple workers were called. Many special experiences were shared.[9]

Houston Texas

Announcement: September 30, 1997

Dedication: August 26-27, 2000
by Gordon B. Hinckley

Site: 11 acres

Floor Area: 33,970 square feet

Exterior Finish: Luna pearl granite

From the *Church News*

In the mid-1980s, when the Houston economy took a downturn, Mr. [Don] Hand was hit so hard that he feared bankruptcy. He prayed to the Lord and begged His assistance, promising to pay Him back in the future. Mr. Hand was spared financial ruin.

As a developer, Mr. Hand originally purchased 2,000 acres in the area [of what is now the Houston Temple site] and had painted a scene for his wife of his conception of the area's future grandeur. The land had been on the market prior to President Gordon B. Hinckley's site-selection trip to Houston, but when he visited the city it was not available. He viewed the location anyway and informed realtor Steve Cook that it was the desired site. However, in response to Brother Cook's queries, Mr. Hand indicated, "No amount of money would interest me in selling that property."

The agent persisted and eventually discussed the intended usage of the land, to build a temple for the Church. Mr. Hand's heart softened. He remembered his promise to the Lord so many years earlier and realized that this would be the perfect opportunity to fulfill it. He agreed to sell.[10]

Birmingham
Alabama

Announcement: September 11, 1998

Dedication: September 3, 2000
by Gordon B. Hinckley

Site: 5.6 acres

Floor Area: 10,700 square feet

Exterior Finish: Imperial Danby white
marble quarried in Vermont

Interesting Facts

- The day before the Birmingham Alabama Temple dedication, Elder David B. Haight was presented with a cake to celebrate his 94th birthday. Elder and Sister Haight celebrated their 70th wedding anniversary the day after the dedication.

- On the day of the groundbreaking ceremony for the Birmingham Alabama Temple, hundreds of members came early and sat patiently in the rain, awaiting the proceedings.

Boston
Massachusetts

Announcement:	September 30, 1995
Dedication:	October 1, 2000 by Gordon B. Hinckley
Site:	8 acres
Floor Area:	69,600 square feet
Exterior Finish:	White granite

Converted by Example

I was born in Guatemala City, Guatemala. I lived there for a short period of time, but when I was three years old, my parents separated and my mother moved us to the United States, seeking a better life.

Growing up in a single-parent household was difficult, and there were many challenges. One thing I was taught at an early age was to have faith in Jesus Christ. My grandmother always said, "Pray to Him in all you do, and He will give you the answer and support you need."

I grew up being a "part-time" Catholic. My grandmother made great efforts to take me to church. We went on days like Easter and Christmas. As I got older, my mother sought to obtain a greater relationship with Jesus Christ. We visited many other churches, but there always seemed to be something that was missing. Despite many opportunities to join other denominations, it just didn't seem right.

I was married at a young age and soon had a son and a daughter. The relationship became abusive until finally my husband and I were separated.

In 2000, I observed my mother travel back and forth to Belmont, Massachusetts, to help in the preparation of an open house for what she called "a temple." She was happy and excited about it and I did not know what it was. I asked her to explain, and she told me

Walking indoors I felt a sense of peace and tranquility that was something I had not experienced in a long time. The end of my shift came much too quickly. I did not want to leave this peaceful place.

that it was a privilege to have one so close to home. She talked about it being the Lord's house and that it was for people who were worthy to enter. She proceeded to invite me to help her at the "open house," a period of time that the building would be open to all visitors. After the open house and dedication, it would only be open to worthy Church members.

I remember thinking that I was not worthy to be helping. I felt like my life was in shambles and I couldn't do it. But I surprised myself when I said yes immediately. I asked for time off of work for the days that I was needed. On the day I was to help, we were shuttled in buses from a garage to the temple. I could feel the excitement around me. Strangely to me, everyone was polite, smiling and, most of all, friendly. I was assigned to help chaperone some tours and was in charge of keeping the end of our group together.

As I observed the care and devotion those serving had, I was greatly moved. The care that people took to place booties on people's feet in order to protect the inside from getting dirty increased my curiosity. I wanted to see what it was like. Walking indoors I felt a sense of peace and tranquility that was something I had not experienced in a long time. The end of my shift came much too quickly. I did not want to leave this peaceful place.

I arranged to have my children come visit on a tour a few days later. My son, eight, and my daughter, three, were excited. My son had an idea of where we were going because they had talked about it at church

when he went with my mom. My daughter did not really understand, or so I thought. She took great care to pick out her "pretty dress." When we arrived and were preparing to enter the inside of the temple, she turned to my grandmother and me and said, "Shhhh…this is Jesus' house." I had not told her where we were or what we were going to see, but she knew. This impression also settled in my heart.

During the months following the open house of the temple, my uncle and his wife invited me weekly to have dinner with them. We went to their house almost each Monday evening. Coincidentally, as they tell it, the missionaries were usually there having dinner and they taught a lesson afterwards. The lessons were interesting to me, but I kept my distance.

The missionaries asked me one Sunday if I wanted to get baptized. My "Yes!" came out before they even finished the question. They asked that I read the Book of Mormon and pray to see if it was true. I told them that I already knew it was true and did not need to pray about it. We took the missionary lessons, and I was baptized with my son on February 18, 2001.

I know that the Lord prepared my heart over a period of many years. He gave me opportunities to stay close to Him. He answered my prayers when I most needed Him. I know with the utmost certainty that this gospel is true. I thank Heavenly Father daily for this marvelous blessing of my conversion.

– Monica Franco-Rivera, Massachusetts

Redlands
California

Announcement: April 21, 2001

Dedication: September 14, 2003
by Gordon B. Hinckley

Site: 4.6 acres

Floor Area: 17,300 square feet

Exterior Finish: Light gray granite

Interesting Facts

- The Redlands California Temple sits on the original Mormon landholdings of the San Bernardino colony, established in 1851 under the direction of President Brigham Young. The ethnically diverse settlement provided colony life to Mormon pioneers, African-American families, Jewish merchants, Spanish rancho families, former Mexican government officials, and local Cahuilla and Serrano Indians.[12]

- Over 15,000 people donated the rocks needed for the temple's construction. Deliveries arrived from local members and out-of-state donors. Some were gathered from the campsite of the 1851 Mormon pioneers, now the Glen Helen Regional Park in Devore.

- Primary children joined the rock project, painting pictures and writing messages on many. The sustained ethnic diversity of the area is evident in the numerous languages represented. The children also donated pennies to help fund the palm trees that circle the temple.[13]

Manhattan New York

Announcement: August 7, 2002

Dedication: June 13, 2004
by Gordon B. Hinckley

Floor Area: 20,630 square feet

Exterior Finish: Granite

Finding Peace

When I found out my fiancé's job was going to take us to the suburbs of New York City, I made the decision to transfer from law school at BYU to Fordham, located in the upper west side of Manhattan. I grew up in a small town, so the decision to move to New York – with its bright lights, yellow taxis, and huge skyscrapers – made me both excited and anxious.

The commute to Fordham took about an hour by train. I managed to navigate through the crowds and subway stops, but there was something about being surrounded by thousands of people I didn't know that made me painfully aware that besides my husband, I really didn't have a single friend out there.

As I heard the subway ding at 66th street, I quickly got off at my stop, and with shaky feet and a nervous heart I began to climb the dingy concrete stairs. I looked up to get my bearings in the morning sunlight and quickly drew in my breath as the first thing I saw was the gleaming statue of Moroni, sitting on top of the Manhattan Temple. Peace flooded my heart and gently reminded me that I wasn't alone – not then,

and not ever. Five years, law school graduation, and three kids later, I have continued to look to the temple, finding peace, purpose, and identity within its walls.

– *Liz Jensen, Utah*

Interesting Facts

- President Gordon B. Hinckley testified of the inspiration of the Lord in locating a temple for the New York City area Saints in Manhattan, noting that the efforts of the previous six years to build a temple in Harrison, New York, had repeatedly met the strong opposition of neighbors.
- In a clever adaptation, the Church gutted and soundproofed the upper and lower floors of its existing multi-function Manhattan building, located across from Lincoln Center, to secure a location for the temple in the city. Just two and a half weeks before the temple's summer dedication, the Church announced that it would be adding a steeple and statue to the building that fall. Hundreds of onlookers filled the streets of Manhattan on Saturday, October 9, 2004, to witness the placement of the 10-foot angel Moroni upon the spire of the temple.
- Door handles shaped like the Statue of Liberty torch are found throughout the Manhattan New York Temple.

San Antonio Texas

Announcement: June 24, 2001

Dedication: May 22, 2005
by Gordon B. Hinckley

Site: 5.5 acres

Floor Area: 16,800 square feet

Exterior Finish: Granite

Where He Walked

When the San Antonio Temple was built, I was so excited to have a temple only five minutes away from my home. I was able to join one of the cleaning teams and really enjoyed the days that I was able to serve by cleaning the rooms of the temple.

One morning, I was one of the first of my team to arrive, and the team supervisor asked me to start in the celestial room. As I made my way down to the beautiful room, it was so quiet and peaceful. No one was talking, and there were no distractions. As I entered the celestial room, I was overcome by the Spirit, and the thought came to my mind that Christ had visited there recently. It was not something I was thinking about previous to entering that room, but the feeling that overcame me was so sweet and so powerful, that I knew the Savior does visit the temples on the earth. They are His houses, they are Holy, and His presence can be felt inside their walls.

They are His houses, they are Holy, and His presence can be felt inside their walls. I will always be grateful for the opportunity to serve in that particular capacity in the San Antonio Temple.

I will always be grateful for the opportunity to serve in that particular capacity in the San Antonio Temple.

The experiences I had there will always be sweet to me, and never forgotten.

– Becky Busath, Ohio

Newport Beach California

Announcement:	April 21, 2001
Dedication:	August 28, 2005 by Gordon B. Hinckley
Site:	8.8 acres
Floor Area:	17,800 square feet
Exterior Finish:	Pink granite from North Carolina

A House for All His Children

In 2005, I had the opportunity to attend the Newport Beach California Temple open house with the young women in my ward. I had never had that chance before and was eager to witness the beauty of the temple, and to see what I had to look forward to when the time came for me to enter it for myself as a worthy member of the Church.

One member of our ward was a young lady who had cerebral palsy and, throughout our growing-up years, had always been included in our activities, despite her inability to really understand what was going on. She had a very young mental capacity and couldn't speak, so she usually made noises or grunts to vocalize her wants and needs, and, as a child tends to do, she would become noisy at some undesirable moments.

I was concerned that, once we entered the more sacred and reverent rooms of the temple, she would be a disturbance to others in our group and outside of our group. However, much to my surprise, as we entered the peaceful and beautiful celestial room, she became completely quiet. We sat and enjoyed the room for a few moments, taking in the breathtaking decor and Spirit there, and as we did so, I observed this young lady. Tears sprung to my eyes as I watched her quietly look around her, and I realized that she was probably conversing with our Heavenly Father in that moment. She was closer to Him at that time than any of us probably realized, and I was humbled by that thought, knowing then and there that this truly was the House of the Lord, a place for us to come and speak with Him and feel close to Him.

– *Kayla Abilez, California*

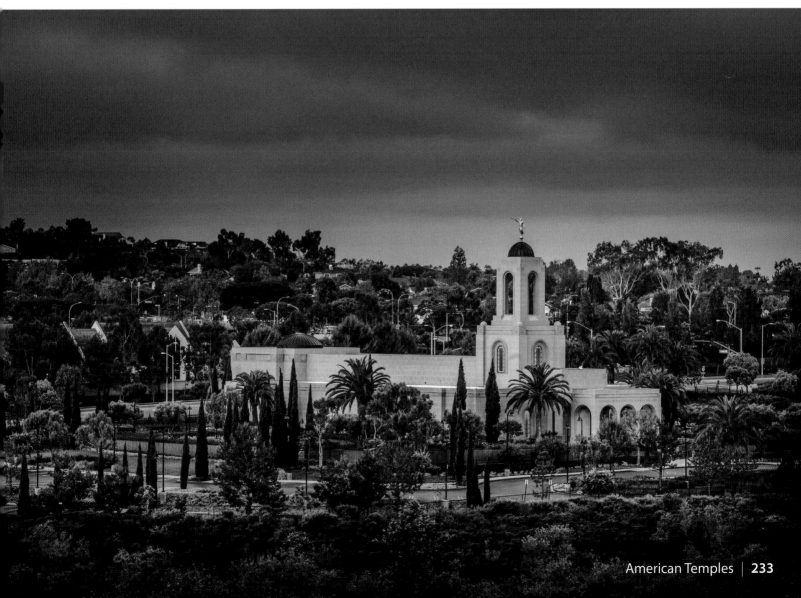

Sacramento
California

Announcement:	April 21, 2001
Dedication:	Sepember 3, 2006 by Gordon B. Hinckley
Site:	46 acres
Floor Area:	19,500 square feet
Exterior Finish:	Granite

From the *Church News*

Plans for building the [Sacramento] temple were met with little resistance by the surrounding communities and government bodies. Many were glad for the building of the temple in the area, because it would improve the land and bring visitors, which would help improve the local economy. The only concern was the height of the temple spire, which the Church agreed to lower twenty feet.

Nearing the completion of the Sacramento California Temple, Okland Construction project manager Russell Mumford reported that the unseasonable weather posed a huge problem. "It rained almost every day for two months, the two months we needed to install the landscaping and finish up the project. Instead of being able to plant, we had a full lake surrounding the temple. The landscape contractor was also frustrated with the situation and pressured by the deadlines. We received permission to invite local members of the Church to participate in the landscaping installation. In 10 days of 4 four-hour shifts and with about 200 volunteers a shift, the orange-vested contractors carefully supervised the crowds of volunteers and the landscaping was completed on time," Mumford explained. "We never could have done it without the local support.[14]

We ask that Thou wilt accept (this temple) as a gift of love for Thee and for Thy Son.

— Gordon B. Hinckley

Rexburg Idaho

Announcement:	December 12, 2003
Dedication:	February 10, 2008 by Thomas S. Monson
Site:	10 acres
Floor Area:	57,504 square feet
Exterior Finish:	Precast concrete with quartz rock finish

Interesting Facts

- While most temple groundbreakings are limited to invited guests, the groundbreaking ceremony for the Rexburg Idaho Temple was open to any and all who desired to attend. Over 8,000 people crowded onto the field where the temple now stands.

- Interest in the open house of the Rexburg Idaho Temple was so high that additional early-morning and evening tours were added to each day. Over 200,000 visitors toured the temple.

- The announcement of the Rexburg Idaho Temple came three and a half years after the announcement that two-year Ricks College would become four-year Brigham Young University–Idaho.

- The Rexburg Idaho Temple dedication was delayed one week due to the passing of President Gordon B. Hinckley on Sunday evening, January 27, 2008.

- President Thomas S. Monson was installed as the 16th president of The Church of Jesus Christ of Latter-day Saints on Sunday, February 3, 2008 – the day originally scheduled for the dedication of the Rexburg Idaho Temple. He dedicated the temple one week later.

Twin Falls Idaho

Announcement: October 2, 2004

Dedication: August 24, 2008
by Thomas S. Monson

Site: 9.1 acres

Floor Area: 31,245 square feet

Exterior Finish: Precast concrete and quartz
rock finish.

From the *Church News*

Throughout the weekend of the [Twin Falls Idaho Temple] dedication, members felt the very personal love of a prophet [President Thomas S. Monson], who often paused to shake hands and converse in his warm and cheerful tones. "Let them feel of Thy divine love and mercy," he asked in his dedicatory prayer. And indeed they did. Following the final dedicatory session, President Monson spent many minutes greeting the smiling Saints who lined the sidewalk from the temple entrance to his awaiting car. When he came upon Maria Eugenia Hernandez, he spoke to her in Spanish, even singing lines from a popular Spanish song with her. Maria was so deeply touched by the experience that for several minutes she could not speak because of her weeping and could not write because of her shaking hands. President Monson's love was returned during his drive to the airport where families lined the roads holding signs that expressed such sentiments as these: "We love the scriptures. We love the prophet. We love the temple."[15]

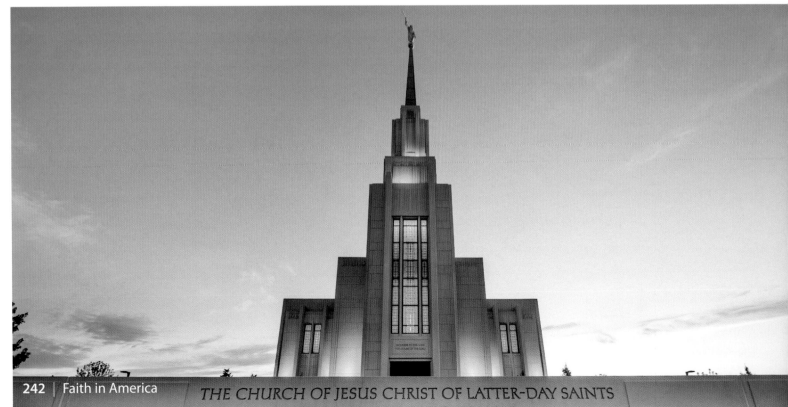

THE CHURCH OF JESUS CHRIST OF LATTER-DAY SAINTS
TWIN FALLS IDAHO TEMPLE

Draper Utah

Announcement:	October 2, 2004
Dedication:	March 20-22, 2009 by Thomas S. Monson
Site:	12 acres
Floor Area:	58,300 square feet
Exterior Finish:	White granite from China

Interesting Facts

- All of the art-glass windows created by Utah artist Tom Holdman for the Draper Utah Temple miraculously survived a fire that left only a portion of one window damaged, even though the art studio itself was so badly burned that it was condemned.

- There are 221 exterior windows, 50 interior windows, and 432 door panels for a total of 35,420 hand-cut pieces of glass. The windows incorporate the Log Cabin quilt pattern used by the early pioneers.

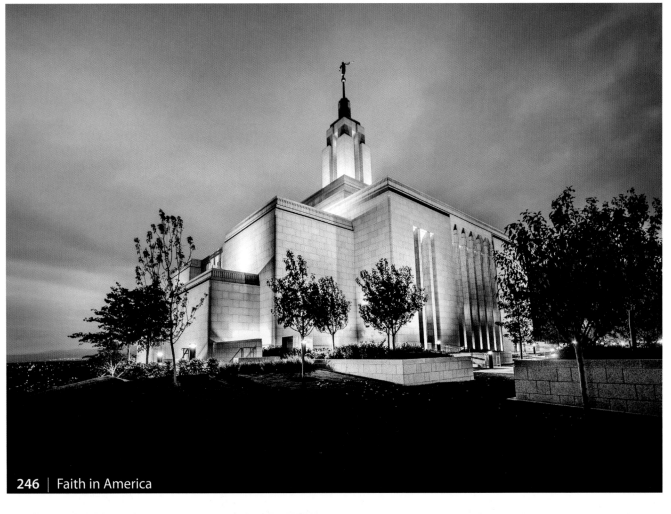

A House of Purity

On one occasion, I volunteered to assist our stake with the assignment to clean the Draper Temple. This cleaning takes place every night after the temple closes.

It is a very thorough cleaning and includes everything from dusting to vacuuming to scrubbing the bathrooms. I felt blessed to receive the assignment to vacuum the second floor, which contains the telestial, terrestrial, celestial, and sealing rooms. Although the whole temple is sacred and holy, these rooms – particularly the celestial room – are especially pure. The reverence that prevails is surreal; and the light, beauty, and spiritual prevalence within those special rooms are incredible.

As I was cleaning, a simple question came to mind: why do they insist that we clean the temple so thoroughly every night? Surely there can't be that much dust and dirt after just one day of use. Why is it so important, I thought to myself, that I vacuum every inch of this carpet, even though there's probably so little dirt that it makes almost no difference? And then the powerful realization struck me: by cleaning the temple day after day, dust has absolutely no chance of collecting and contaminating the cleanliness of the holy house.

If we postponed our daily cleaning, the temple would, at times, be found dirty and impure. Of course, this realization is an obvious one; however, I immediately realized its application to our individual lives. How often do we postpone the 'cleaning up' of our lives because we don't visibly see the dirt of sin which stains us? Are we applying the atoning blood of Christ in our lives constantly to prevent sin from accumulating and tarnishing our souls? Or are we letting miniscule amounts of dirt – even the things of the world – slowly creep into our lives and build up until we can see the stain of sin upon us? Repentance is a beautiful process of renovation and purification which each of us direly needs on a daily basis.

And then the powerful realization struck me: by cleaning the temple day after day, dust has absolutely no chance of collecting and contaminating the cleanliness of the holy house.

We should not wait for the filth of sin to accumulate in our lives; rather, let us keep ourselves pure and clean through the Atonement of Jesus Christ, striving constantly to emulate His perfect life and "receive His image in [our] countenances" (Alma 5:14). The temple serves as a constant reminder to us that we should live our lives in such a way that we may be found worthy to enter the House of the Lord, and ultimately, His presence.

May we set a personal goal that our personal purity and cleanliness can reflect the purity and cleanliness of the temple, as we supplicate in prayer to our loving Father, "More holiness give me" (Hymns, 131).

– *Alex J. Olson, Utah*

Oquirrh Mountain
Utah

Announcement: October 1, 2005

Dedication: August 21-23, 2009
by Thomas S. Monson

Site: 11 acres

Floor Area: 60,000 square feet

Exterior Finish: Beige granite from China

Open House Touches Hearts

Our family was one of many who had the privilege of volunteering at the Oquirrh Mountain Temple during the open house in 2009. My job was to stand and direct visitors as they quietly walked through. Thousands of people participated in the open house, and it was surprisingly fulfilling to be able to simply look each person in the eye and smile – and to find that almost everyone smiled back. There is an unmistakable Spirit there, and I know hearts were touched.

We invited a family to the open house, and they readily accepted our invitation. Though it wasn't required, they chose to dress in their Sunday best – even their little daughters – and they seemed to feel the Spirit strongly as they toured. Years later, they asked about attending another Utah temple dedication, and we have promised to take them through the Payson and Provo City Center Temples as soon as they are open. I hope that someday they'll be able to enter a dedicated temple and experience the great joy of becoming an eternal family.

I'm thankful for the blessings the temple has brought to me and my family. My two daughters have now been through the Oquirrh Mountain Temple, one when she was married and the other in preparation for her mission, and I look forward to the time when my two boys will be able to have those same sweet experiences in the House of the Lord.

It was surprisingly fulfilling to be able to simply look each person in the eye and smile – and to find that almost everyone smiled back.

– *Karen Hyatt, Utah*

The Plan of Salvation taught in the temple with simplicity, yet with power, will be as a never-failing beacon of divine light to guide our footsteps and keep them constantly on the pathway of eternal life.

– Thomas S. Monson

Gila Valley
Arizona

Announcement: April 26, 2008

Dedication: May 23, 2010
by Thomas S. Monson

Site: 17 acres

Floor Area: 18,561 square feet

Exterior Finish: Precast stone

Interesting Facts

- The groundbreaking ceremony for The Gila Valley Arizona Temple was held on the 97th anniversary of Arizona's becoming a state.

- The shovels were specially arranged so that ground was broken at the location where the Celestial Room would stand.

- President Thomas S. Monson's announcement of the construction of The Gila Valley Arizona Temple and the Gilbert Arizona Temple was his first temple announcement as president of The Church of Jesus Christ of Latter-day Saints.

May faith increase in the hearts of all who come, and may a knowledge of Thy eternal plan grow in the minds of those who here serve, be they workers or patrons.

— Thomas S. Monson

Kansas City Missouri

Announcement: October 4, 2008

Dedication: May 6, 2012
by Thomas S. Monson

Site: 8.05 acres

Floor Area: 32,000 square feet

Exterior Finish: Concrete

We Get a Temple!

Conference Saturday, October 2008. I was at work as a rural mail carrier sub, working on a route that included an LDS chapel. There was no mailbox on this chapel (mail is sent to the homes of Church leaders) so the regular carrier sends back anything mailed to the chapel with the label, "No mail receptacle." A letter came that day, from a distant state, for the family history center in that building. I was thinking the big miracle of the day was that I was doing that route and it was conference Saturday, so I knew I could get the letter to someone.

I got to the church five minutes after the morning session ended and asked a couple, who were heading to their car, if there was a member of a bishopric around. They pointed to someone leaving on a motorcycle and flagged him down. I gave him the letter, and he said he would get it to the right people. I was thinking about how amazing it would be if I did some little thing to help some name get to a temple.

As I headed back to my postal vehicle, I passed the same couple and said casually, "So did I miss anything good this morning?"

The wife replied, "We get a temple!"

I stopped in my tracks and we grabbed each other by the hands and started jumping up and down and screaming. *Screaming.*

I finally let go and said, "I'm sorry, you don't even know me." I told her my name and she told me hers and we grabbed each other again and started jumping and screaming. The euphoria lasted all day.

The next day I went to my chapel to watch the Sunday morning session. I found the man who records the sessions and told him I just wanted to see that announcement for myself. He went into the library and cued it up on a TV for me to watch later. After the morning session he announced, "Celeste would like to see the temple announcement, so it is ready in the library. If anyone missed it or would like to see it again, we are going to watch it now." Every single person in the chapel crowded into the library, and we were all hugging each other and crying.

The power of the announcement was only the beginning. It felt like a celebration from the announcement to the dedication day.

– *Celeste Reed, Montana*

> *I told her my name and she told me hers and we grabbed each other again and started jumping and screaming. The euphoria lasted all day.*

Brigham City
Utah

Announcement:	October 3, 2009
Dedication:	September 23, 2012 by Boyd K. Packer
Site:	3.14 acres
Floor Area:	36,000 square feet
Exterior Finish:	Precast concrete

From the *Church News*

"I am home," said President Boyd K. Packer in his opening remarks at the Brigham City Utah Temple groundbreaking held Saturday, July 31, 2010. President Packer, president of the Quorum of the Twelve Apostles, and his wife Donna are natives of Brigham City.

President Packer had attended elementary school 80 years before on the very site where he stood. He continued, "I can see in my mind's eye a temple sitting here in about two years' time. It will be gorgeous, it will be white. You will see in the design of it reflections of previous temples that have been built, particularly the Salt Lake Temple. It will be a beacon from all over the valley."[16]

Gilbert Arizona

Announcement:	April 26, 2008
Dedication:	March 2, 2014 by Thomas S. Monson (read by Henry B. Eyring)
Site:	15.83 acres
Floor Area:	85,326 square feet

Behind the Scenes

Under a beautiful blue Arizona sky, the Gilbert Arizona Temple was dedicated to the Lord Sunday, March 2, 2014. It was the perfect bookend to the months of planning and work necessary to prepare the temple for its dedication. I had served on the temple dedication committee and chaired the physical facilities subcommittee. My wife, Janna, and I had the opportunity to attend the first dedicatory session in the temple. As we were ushered through the front door and to our assigned seats, I thought of the countless hours the members of my committee and I had spent inside of the temple over the past two months cleaning, moving furniture, and doing various other tasks associated with the open house and dedication. This day, my eyes were lifted from the physical to the spiritual as I contemplated the importance and meaning of the temple. I felt such a connection with the temple. All who had served felt the same. This was our temple – we had given our time, talents, energy, and sweat preparing the temple for this day. I loved the relationship I felt with my God because I had sacrificed for something that would be so important to thousands of Heavenly Father's children.

The work leading up to the dedication was significant and, at times, quite challenging. I cannot begin to articulate all that was accomplished by the amazing volunteers who served. Through it all, I gained a great appreciation for the unsung heroes of

> *I gained a great appreciation for the unsung heroes of the Church – those people who dilligently work behind the scenes…that keep things running.*

the Church – those people who diligently work behind the scenes taking care of the seemingly small and mundane (and at times very distasteful) jobs that keep things running.

Over 400,000 people attended the open house and walked through the temple and the stake center next door. And about 6,000 people attended one of the three dedicatory sessions for the temple, including the cornerstone ceremony. All of these activities required a small army of dedicated Latter-day Saints who willingly took on the unglamorous jobs, endured numerous challenges, and solved problems. They did this work with joy because they loved the Lord and wanted to consecrate themselves to build the kingdom. I hope I am always willing to perform whatever is asked, regardless of the task, that I may learn how to be a better disciple of Jesus Christ.

– *Jason Bagley, Arizona*

A Place of Miracles

My husband and I were asked to be "tour guides" in our native Spanish language for the four weeks that the Gilbert Temple open house would be taking place. This is an amazing opportunity to meet people that are not members of the Church, to share our beliefs, and to explain why temples are so sacred to us. We enjoyed attending once every week and taking several groups of people through the beautiful rooms of the temple. My favorite part was to see their faces when we entered the celestial room; their expressions were so touching. It was such a privilege to be there in such a special place, enjoying the Spirit and doing missionary work.

Because of our schedule, we had chosen to go every Saturday, and on February 8th, our shift began at 5:00 p.m. This would have been our third time volunteering, but as we walked across the street to the temple, two cars crashed behind us, causing one of them to lose control and come straight toward us. Just a couple of steps away from the sidewalk, my husband was pushed away, and I was left trapped under the car.

I slipped into a coma, and skull fractures, several broken ribs, brain trauma, and other issues were news to me when I woke up in the hospital two weeks later. The last memory I had of that day was when we had arrived and parked our car to serve in the temple. How sad I was when I found out the date and learned that our time as tour guides was over.

My heart is full of gratitude to everyone that, in one way or another, helped us. There was always an army of angels taking care of my family. What a wonderful experience this has been to witness the miracle of healing and brotherhood! One minute I was ready to share my feelings of the gospel with others, of how happy we can feel when we follow Jesus Christ, and of the blessings of the temple that we can receive in this life and for eternity; the next minute, I became the recipient of those same feelings and blessings through the kind acts of hundreds of friends and family.

I am a good 80 percent recovered, against a lot of negative possibilities. I can hear, walk, talk, remember, and do everything almost as if it didn't happen. With the help of therapy, I face a hopeful future.

I know the temple is the House of the Lord, and I have a testimony that it's the highest, most sacred place in this lowly world. To me, the Gilbert Arizona Temple is a place of miracles. God preserved my life there; He also touched the hearts of the people that toured through the temple during the open house (last month we attended the baptism of a family member that we were fortunate enough to show the temple to), and because miracles have not ceased to happen, God is a God of miracles!

– *Laura Laparra Rivera, Arizona*

Fort Lauderdale
Florida

Announcement:	October 3, 2009
Dedication:	May 4, 2014 by Dieter F. Uchtdorf
Site:	16.82 acres
Floor Area:	30,500 square feet
Exterior Finish:	Architectural designed concrete

Miracles Each Day

A sizable number of open house guests left the Church's 143rd temple having experienced something entirely unexpected. "They walked away from the [Fort Lauderdale Florida] temple with a great change in their heart," said Miami Lakes Florida Stake President James Robinson. "Some asked if they could become members. Others have said they wanted to be married inside the temple."

Miracles, said President Robinson, have marked each day at the temple.

"We've had some members who have served every day during the open house and others who have served whenever they can," President Robinson said. "Some of our volunteers don't have cars, and they've walked miles each day to volunteer at the temple." [17]

A Trip Well Taken

As converts to the Lord's Church, my husband and I wanted to start our marriage with the blessing of being sealed in the Lord's House for time and eternity with our first daughter. In the year 2000, we entered the Orlando Florida Temple to be sealed as a couple, and then to be sealed as a family for time and all eternity. That day was a beautiful and spiritual day that we will never forget; however, fourteen years later, a greater blessing came to our family, when we were able to participate with our children in the Fort Lauderdale Florida Temple open house.

We traveled from Tampa to Fort Lauderdale on a trip of four and a half hours. Early Saturday morning, my family and I started getting anxious with excitement to get into the temple and participate in the open house tour; nevertheless, none of us were prepared for what unfolded next. As we approached the temple, our hearts started jumping out of our chests. The kids did not mind the long trip or the muddy area near the temple parking lot. All of us just wanted to get inside and see it.

What a marvelous experience and faith building time we had that day. We all loved the temple tour, and we were in awe of the beauty of each room, the outside of the temple, and its gardens. The two rooms in which my kids wanted to stay longer were the celestial room and the brides' room; each of my girls wanted to stay and daydream a little longer about when they would enter for their special day. The mirrors and the beauty of that big light blue chandelier in the brides' room made them believe they were real princesses in a beautiful castle. Each one of them was contemplating the majesty, peace, and beauty promised in the House of the Lord. This made them want to work hard and become worthy of entering the temple one day, to be endowed, and to be sealed to their spouses for all time and all eternity.

Though the temple was not yet dedicated, the Spirit of the Lord was felt everywhere, and it touched each one of us very deeply in our souls. What a marvelous experience to be able to share it with my babies and my husband; it was as if we were entering as a family in the eternal mansions of Heaven and staying there forever. As parents, we looked forward to the day when we would see each of our children accomplishing that beautiful promise of love to the Lord, to us, and to their spouses. I pray for the day and the blessing in which I get to share again with the love of my life, with all my six kids and all my future generations, the love, peace and happiness that we felt that day.

– Maria Luisa Vasquez, Florida

Payson Utah

Kirtland Ohio

Canadian Temples

Cardston Alberta

Edmonton Alberta

Calgary Alberta

Index

Temples

Albuquerque New Mexico, 166-169

Anchorage Alaska, 140-143

Atlanta Georgia, 80-83

Baton Rouge Louisiana, 192-195

Billings Montana, 154-159

Birmingham Alabama, 202-203

Bismarck North Dakota, 150-151

Boise Idaho, 84-87

Boston Massachusetts, 204-207

Bountiful Utah, 120-123

Brigham City Utah, 262-265

Canadian Temples, 276-277

Chicago Illinois, 92-95

Columbia River Washington, 212-213

Columbia South Carolina, 150-151

Columbus Ohio, 146-147

Dallas Texas, 88-91

Denver Colorado, 96-99

Detroit Michigan, 152-153

Draper Utah, 246-249

Fort Lauderdale Florida, 270-273

Fresno California, 178-179

Gila Valley Arizona, 254-257

Gilbert Arizona, 266-269

Houston Texas, 198-201

Idaho Falls Idaho, 42-45

Jordan River Utah, 76-79

Kansas City Missouri, 258-261

Kirtland Ohio, 275

Kona Hawaii, 162-165

Laie Hawaii, 34-37

Las Vegas Nevada, 104-109

Logan Utah, 16-21

Los Angeles California, 46-51

Louisville Kentucky, 170-171

Lubbock Texas, 216-217

Manhattan New York, 226-227

Manti Utah, 22-27

Medford Oregon, 180-183

Memphis Tennessee, 184-185

Mesa Arizona, 38-41

Monticello Utah, 138-139

Mount Timpanogos Utah, 124-129

Nashville Tennessee, 192-193

Nauvoo Illinois, 218-223

Newport Beach California, 230-233

Oakland California, 52-57

Ogden Utah, 58-61

Oklahoma City Oklahoma, 196-197

Oquirrh Mountain Utah, 250-253

Orlando Florida, 116-119

Palmyra New York, 172-177

Payson Utah, 274

Portland Oregon, 100-103

Provo Utah, 62-65

Raleigh North Carolina, 160-161

Redlands California, 224-225

Reno Nevada, 186-189

Rexburg Idaho, 238-241

Sacramento California, 234-237

St. George Utah, 12-15

St. Louis Missouri, 130-133

St. Paul Minnesota, 162-163

Salt Lake City Utah, 28-33

San Antonio Texas, 228-229

San Diego California, 110-115

Seattle Washington, 72-75

Snowflake Arizona, 214-215

Spokane Washington, 144-145

Twin Falls Idaho, 242-245

Vernal Utah, 134-137

Washington D.C., 66-71

Winter Quarters Nebraska, 208-211

Authors

Abilez, Kayla (Newport Beach) 231

Allen, Denise (Manti) 24

Anderson, D. (Washington D.C.) 69

Bagley, Jason (Gilbert) 266-267

Baird, Austin (Lubbock) 217

Barnett, Elaine (St. Louis) 132

Bingham, Kathleen (Provo) 64

Boyack, Connor (San Diego) 113

Busath, Becky (San Antonio) 228

Butler, Shay (Idaho Falls) 44

Carter, Bernadene A. (Atlanta) 83

Clevenstine, Sharron (Boise) 86

Coleman, Kaylene Myres (Anchorage) 142

Cozzens, Carri (Monticello) 138

Doutre'Jones, Richard (San Diego) 113

Ethington, Meredith (Los Angeles) 48

Franco-Rivera, Monica (Boston) 204-207

Galbraith, Rachel Whitaker (Mt. Timp) 126

Garvin, Kristin (Orlando) 116

Geambaşu, Izabela (Salt Lake) 30

Greene, Carrie (Oakland) 54-55

Grimske, Eivonny Yvonne (Loisville) 170-171

Herbert, Carmen Rasmusen (Bountiful) 123

Hyatt, Karen (Oquirrh Mountain) 250

Jensen, Liz (Manhattan) 227

Lemmon, Kayla (Salt Lake) 32

Lines, Derek (Albuquerque) 166-168

Moulton, Deanna (Fresno) 178

Olson, Alex J. (Draper) 249

Quirante, Benjeline Misalucha (Dallas) 90

Reed, Celeste (Kansas City) 261

Ropte, Shelbee (Las Vegas) 107

Self, Danielle (Seattle) 74

Sorensen, Beau (St. George) 15

Steenhoek, David (Los Angeles) 51

Stirling, Lindsey (Mesa) 40

Toney, Ben (Bountiful) 121

Vasquez, Maria Luisa (Fort Lauderdale) 272

Voss, James (Denver) 99

Weber, Stephen (Nauvoo) 220-221

Wilkes, Daniel (Medford) 180

Wright, Rebecca Brown (Jordan River) 79

References

(Interesting Facts and Dedicatory Prayers) Satterfield, Rick. Ldschurchtemples.com. January 1, 1998.

(Interesting Facts) Mormontemples.com. January 1, 2014.

1. Holman, Marianne. "'In Grandpa's Footsteps' - Walking to the Logan Utah Temple." *Church News*, July 7, 2012.

2. Borrowman, Jerry. "Centenarian to Spend His 100th Birthday at Idaho Falls Temple." *Deseret News*, May 3, 2012.

3. Van Orden, Dell. "Shortening the Vast Distance." *Church News*, September 25, 1999.

4. Hill, Greg. "A Temple in Their Midst." *Church News*, 30 October 1999.

5. Hill, Greg. "Blessing for Saints of Montana, Wyoming" *Church News*, 27 November 1999.

6. Lloyd, R. Scott. "While Building Temple, He Embraced the Gospel" *Church News*, 25 December 1999.

7. Kruckenberg, Janet. "Ground Broken for Temple in Minnesota" *Church News*, 3 October 1998.

8. Dockstader, Julie. "Reno Temple: Easter Day Dedication Brings Hope." *Church News*, April 29, 2000.

9. Christensen, Emily. "Family History Mission Leads to Family, Ward Blessings for One Convert." *Deseret News*, August 25, 2013.

10. *Church News*, June 20, 1998.

11. "Leaders Break Ground, Offer Counsel at Temple Site in Snowflake, Ariz.", *Church News*, September 30, 2000.

12. Marilyn Mills, "Video Teaches Diverse History," *Church News*, 16 Aug. 2003: 3.

13. "Redlands Temple in Inland Empire: President Hinckley Dedicates Edifice near San Bernardino Mountains," *Church News*, 20 Sept. 2003: 3.

14. "The Work of Temple Construction," *Church News*, 27 Aug. 2009

15. Gerry Avant, "New Temple is Dedicated in Idaho," *Church News*, 30 Aug. 2008: 3.

16. The Church of Jesus Christ of Latter-day Saints News Release, "President Packer Presides at Groundbreaking of Brigham City Utah Temple," 31 Jul. 2010.

17. Swensen, Jason. *Deseret News*, April 19, 2014.